SIMKIN'S SOLDIERS
THE BRITISH ARMY IN 1890

VOLUME II
The Infantry

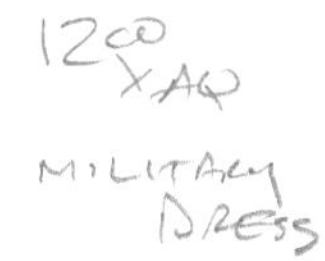

SIMKIN'S SOLDIERS

THE BRITISH ARMY IN 1890

VOLUME II
The Infantry

Colonel P S Walton
late Royal Army Ordnance Corps

With a Foreword by
General Sir Michael Gow GCB

PICTON PUBLISHING (CHIPPENHAM) LTD

Copyright 1986 P. S. Walton
First published by
Picton Publishing (Chippenham) Ltd 1987

ISBN 0 948251 02 6

Printed in Great Britain by
Picton Print
Citadel Works
Bath Road
Chippenham
Wiltshire SN15 2AB
PP52241

CONTENTS

THE PLATES

FOREWORD
by General Sir Michael Gow GCB

In my Foreword to Volume I, I described "Simkin's Soldiers" as a "deeply researched work of great erudition", and I have no hesitation in repeating that with regard to Volume II. This is a fascinating book and as an Infantryman myself I found it not only extremely interesting but also a fund of information. Colonel Walton deals with every facet from organisation and equipment through to the minutiae of dress, and I was amazed by my ignorance.

Once again it is beautifully illustrated, and the colour plates of Richard Simkin's pictures are admirable.

This, therefore, is not merely a book for those whose interest lies only in uniforms, but it is also for anyone who wishes to learn about that branch of the Army which was and still is, as Colonel Walton says, "the Foundation".

Royal College of Defence Studies
January 1986

INTRODUCTION

When I began this work, I was well aware of the blind alleys, traps and pitfalls awaiting the researcher. But I was not so well prepared for the trials and tribulations of printing and publishing. It is now all history but the basis upon which Volume I came out has disappeared. With it went the original timetable for Volume II and the plan for its contents; instead of being based upon twenty-two original watercolours, it has now been restricted to eighteen to match Volume I. They all feature regiments of infantry in order to try to do justice to that arm. After this I have every hope of producing a third and final volume, a main objective of which will be to cover the Royal Engineers and the Departmental Corps.

In the introduction to Volume I, I explained the origin of this book and its purpose. Briefly it was to expose to the student of military affairs of the era, whether academic, soldier or modeller, some of the best of Richard Simkin's work. The plates are taken from the originals for the very well-known Army and Navy Gazette series of prints. Most of these water-colour drawings were done between 1888 and 1892, the beginning of the artist's best period. While by no means free from error, they are nonetheless pretty accurate and they are certainly very pleasing pictures. They compare most favourably with the old prints, and this is particularly so where the Scottish Regiments are concerned. Unjust coals have been heaped for many years on the head of the unfortunate Simkin for the crimes of the engraver and colourist employed by the Army and Navy Gazette's printer. A quick comparison between the print and the original as reproduced here will show up differences to the advantage, I believe, of the artist.

The coloured plates are pleasant pictures but they do not by themselves give full information. As I explained in Volume I, I therefore set myself the task of complementing them with sufficient supporting material for the student to see what soldiers of the day actually did and wore. Yet, if only for lack of space this could not be a comprehensive study and where uniforms are concerned, descriptions and drawings are generally confined to those which appear in the coloured plates. I make no apology for the sometimes uneven treatment which has resulted and I have digressed towards a fuller coverage in several areas. For example, I have made an attempt to list non-commissioned ranks with some of the more common appointments and the associated badges. While this is an advance on Volume I which I hope will be of value, I must emphasise that the subject is complex; the lists should there-fore be regarded as illustrative and in no sense as comprehensive. Similarly, I have devoted rather more than their due proportion of space and illustrations to the Scottish Regiments. Such information as there is in print about their dress tends, I think, to assume that the reader knows all about

Highland garb; I, for one, did not. Nonetheless, the identification and description of items of uniform together with an accurate account of when and how they were worn remain a real minefield for the unwary. The watchword, therefore, and I strongly emphasise it, is: "assume nothing"!

Several aspects of the British military scene about 1890 deserve explanation. In 1881, the infantry were subjected to the Cardwell reorganisation which linked many old single-battalion Regiments in pairs to form new Regiments. Many marriages were grudgingly entered into and a few were down-right resisted. Some of the flavour of this unhappy process finds its way into the book. Those who have served in the British Army since 1958 have observed or experienced two further bouts of similar forced marriages, and the odd voluntary disbandment (which many condemned but most secretly admire). Readers in the United States where the "unit" to which loyalty is due is often the Division rather than the Battalion may have difficulty in understanding the strength of feeling engendered by any attempt to tamper with a British Regiment's household gods. If so, read on! They may also be confused by the way in which Battle Honours have been shown in the Regimental sections. Each list is correct up to 1890 and the Honours are listed in sequence of award. Where two different pre-Cardwell parent Regiments were concerned, relevance is indicated by e.g. (1) for the senior, in the left-hand column. Where exceptionally the Honour was won by both parent Regiments but awarded on different dates, both are shown. I should also explain that while I have taken some care to list the family history of those Regiments I have chosen to illustrate, I have not included any other disbanded and quite unconnected unit which may previously have held such a Regiment's number. Regimental establishments are taken from Army Orders and the relevant strength figures together with the locations from the official returns for April 1890. In the text I have used abbreviations; these are explained in Appendix II which has been expanded from Volume I. Similarly, I have referred to other works by means of a figure in brackets, e.g. (6) which relates to its serial number in the expanded bibliography at Appendix III.

For those who want to know more about Richard Simkin, there is a note on him in Volume I. Two volumes of his later drawings have been published recently (22) and these contain more information. Apart from the colour plates, the vignettes in the text of the present book are by Simkin and as in Volume I are reproduced from juvenilia of the 1880s.

In putting this volume together I have been very much encouraged by messages of interest and support from members of the Victorian Military Society and others all over the world. I am sorry to have kept them waiting. I have tried to imagine the questions they would all ask; I hope that I have unlocked at least some of the answers. If I have failed, or got it wrong anywhere, I hope that readers will let me know. My comments or corrections will all be published, as with Volume I, in the Journal of the Victorian Military Society. In short, to research is to publish: I dedicate this volume to you who read the result in the hope that study in this bewitching field will give you as much pleasure as it has given to me.

Acknowledgements

This volume would not have appeared now, if at all, without the confidence and practical support of David Picton-Phillips, my publisher. To him, therefore, go my warmest thanks. But both he and I owe much – dare I say it – to Anne his wife for unremitting hard work on sales and book-keeping, not to mention a hot kitchen stove. I have reason to appreciate both and I take this opportunity to thank her too.

I wrote Volume I in Germany; I wrote some of this volume in Zimbabwe. Neither place is particularly suitable for studying the British Army of 100 years ago. I am therefore all the more grateful to those hard-pressed members of institutions, including Regimental HQs, who have so generously given me of their time and knowledge. I particularly wish to mention Mr Bill Boag of the Scottish United Services Museum and Lt Col David Murray for their friendly and voluminous advice on the mysteries of Scottish military dress; Lt Col Jack Reilly, Lt Col John Bottomley, Mr Norman Holme, Mr John Willoughby, Lt Col Ralph May and Mr Stephen Shannon kindly provided photographs and advice concerning respectively the Royal Inniskilling Fusiliers, Green Howards, Royal Welch Fusiliers, Oxfordshire Light Infantry, Border Regiment and the Durham Light Infantry. I acknowledge the permission of the Green Howards to reproduce an extract from their Regimental magazine, and I am grateful to the owners of photographs for permission to reproduce them. Capt David Horn of RHQ Grenadier Guards checked the Foot Guards section of the manuscript; Major Donald Baxter kindly helped me out with specific information about the Northamptons; Lt Col Reggie Pratt and latterly Mr Tom Hewitson advised me about the Northumberland Fusiliers; Lt Col Christopher Wolverson and the Officers of 1st Bn The King's Own Royal Border Regiment allowed me to look at their French drums. I also thank Mr Peter Boyden of The National Army Museum, and Mr Potts and Mrs Blacklaw of the Ministry of Defence Library, for their diligence in finding items in their care and helping me freely from their knowledge and experience. In addition I would like to take this opportunity of thanking a number of friends and fellow students of what I call "military antecedents" (I do not like the term "militaria" which rhymes too easily with hysteria) for their support and help; in particular I thank Mr John Thomson of Edinburgh, Major George Bush of Perryville, Missouri, and Mr Ron Harris of Southsea.

As with Volume I, my special thanks are due to the staff of the Army Museums Ogilby Trust. The Trust's collection of photographs is unique and invaluable, and I am grateful to Col Pip Newton for permission to use those I needed; I am most grateful to John Tamplin and Alf Flatow for their advice and hospitality during several visits. Finally, although the owner of the original watercolours reproduced in this book wishes to remain anonymous, I am naturally most grateful for his permission to use them; without them, there would be little indeed to show the reader.

The manuscript was expertly typed by Mrs Melanie Boyce and Mrs Mary Pugson and the photographs were skilfully produced by Mr Alan Lawley of Linton Studio, Cambridge. I am grateful to them all. Lastly, I thank my wife for her encouragement and indeed for her determination that this volume should finally see the light of day.

Andover
June 1986

List of Illustrations

Figures

Note: In old photographs, yellow and red did not stand out as light shades in the way that they do under modern processing. Similarly, different grades of cloth of the same colour in the same photograph tended to show up as different colours.

List of Illustrations

Colour Plates

THE INFANTRY

The infantry are the foundation of the British Army. Their duty has always been to capture and hold ground and, in the final analysis, this is the key to war. Even today despite the power of nuclear weapons and the tactical glamour of tanks and helicopters, this remains essentially true. The Army of 1890 was not of course properly tested until 1899 and when the time came it did not do too well at first. There were many reasons for this. For example, a glance at the (drill and) tactical manual of the day, Infantry Drill 1889, betrays the fact that "fire and manouevre", in the sense that is fundamental today, was a technique still to be learned. Yet while one may wonder how the stereotyped and unimaginative drills laid out could have been expected to be effective, one can only applaud the Army Order printed as a preface to the manual, in which Lord Wolseley remarks:

"These regulations are based on the principle of demanding great exactitude in the simplified movements still retained for Drill, while conceding the utmost latitude to all commanders, of however small a unit, in Manoeuvre. The first must be carried out literally, the second must be observed in the spirit more than in the letter."

Company field training was programmed formally and lasted for up to a month every year. The syllabus was laid down in *(20)* Infantry Drill 1889 Part X Sections 18 and 19 and includes, besides tactical manoeuvres, map-reading for NCOs and duties such as those of advance and rear guards, working parties, reconnoitring, outpost duties and camping. At the end, every man had to be accounted for in terms of attendance and performance in a return made not merely to the CO but to the GOC himself. This matched the system for reporting the results of the annual course of musketry training which was mandatory for all except Staff Sergeants, men with over twenty-one years' service and recruits. Field training, in short, was taken seriously by the Army at this time. Everything was done so far as possible as it was believed it would be done on active service. For example, tents did not accompany a marching battalion and officers were restricted to 40lb baggage each. But the strict discipline which was such a strength in the maintenance of relatively simple standards was also a weakness because it inhibited the development of that initiative for which Lord Wolseley was surely feeling in his preface to the Manual. Unthinking discipline lacks resilience and generally fails in the end. So it was that nine years later, on the eve of the 2nd South African War, we find *(1)* that standards had slipped. As an illustration some battalions could not go on manoeuvres (we would now call it "exercise" or "field training exercise" FTX) without a hospital marquee for the Officers' Mess with dining table, chairs and all the trimmings. Not only was this poor training but it was also very expensive as civilian carriers had to be hired to move all this impedimenta about the country. Did that have anything to do with our showing in South Africa? Perhaps not directly, but indirectly it must have contributed by encouraging an attitude of mind which was at best dated. It needed the dramatic and distressing events of Black Week 1899 to get training back onto realistic and progressive lines.

1 *Types of the York and Lancaster Regiment circa 1892*

Organisation and Training

As in the Cavalry, the Infantry included a number of Regiments who were Household troops; the remainder and the vast majority were referred to as the "Line". The Household infantry were the three Regiments of Foot Guards illustrated in this book with, between them, seven regular battalions. The regular line consisted of 141 battalions found by sixty-seven territorial Regiments and two Rifle Regiments without geographic affiliation. The latter shared a depot at Winchester but the others each had their own depot of which forty-five were in England, three in Wales, eleven in Scotland and the remaining eight were in Ireland. The depot and the Regimental district within which it lay and from which in general it drew its recruits, was commanded by a Colonel. Associated with it but each under their own CO were the Militia and Volunteer battalions of the Regiment; these were part-time soldiers and their role, training and dress is unfortunately beyond the capacity of this volume to describe. At the head of the Regimental family was its Colonel, a distinguished senior officer in many cases retired from the active list.

Every Regiment had two regular battalions except the Rifle Regiments with four each and the Queen's Own Cameron Highlanders with, at this period, only one. The disposition of the Line was broadly on the principle of one regular battalion at home and the other abroad. They changed over on average about every sixteen years while the home battalion changed station about every two years. At this period, the Foot Guards did not go overseas in peacetime, which was a disadvantage as the total number of infantry battalions abroad exceeded those at Home by eleven; there were fifty-three in India and twenty-three in the Colonies but only sixty-five in the United Kingdom. The result was that several Regiments had both battalions abroad and therefore a larger depot from which to "feed" them. Between September and March each year was the so-called "Trooping Season" when drafts were dispatched from the home battalion to its "foreign" sister. They were to replace time-expired men as well as the inevitable casualties of active service, accident and sickness. A draft was usually at least 100 non-commissioned ranks none of whom were to be below twenty years of age nor with less than eighteen months' service. They were, in short, expected to be trained mature soldiers and it was for this reason that the home battalion was known as "the school of the Regiment". There were also other and less reverent names which indicated how strongly some people felt about this constant "milking" process!

There was considerable variety in battalion establishments but in principle the organisation of all was the same. Battalion HQ with about eight officers and the two WOs of those days (the Sergeant-Major and the Bandmaster) controlled the corporate affairs of eight companies. Each of these was commanded by a Major or a Captain with two or three other officers, a Colour Sergeant, three or four Sergeants, four or five Corporals, two Drummers and 85–110 Lance Corporals and Privates. A company was divided into half-companies commanded by a subaltern officer and each of those into two Sections under a Sergeant or a Corporal. Operating in Battalion HQ were the Adjutant with the Orderly Room Clerks, the Quartermaster and his storemen, the Signalling Officer and his small group of not less than eight, the Pioneer Sergeant and his ten men and, in certain battalions only, the battalion transport and the mounted infantry (of which more on page 17). Other specialists in the battalion included the Bandmaster and his musicians, the Sergeant-Instructor of Musketry, the Armourer-Sergeant (attached from the Corps of Armourers) and the medical team. The latter consisted of an NCO and two men per company trained as first-aiders and stretcher-bearers. Battalions generally had no medical officer nor even a qualified orderly; other than in India, where a doctor was sometimes attached to a unit, the policy was to concentrate the medical resources in each Garrison into the Station Hospital.

Recruiting standards and engagements varied between Guards and Line. The former looked for men with a minimum height of 5ft 9in and a chest measurement of 34 inches. The minimum standards for the Line were 5ft 4in in height and a chest measurement of a mere 33 inches – a terrible comment by today's standards on the social conditions of the age. The engagement upon enlistment was for twelve years; in the Line this was made up of seven years with the Colours and five on the Reserve, while in the Foot Guards it was three and nine. In both cases, naturally, soldiers could extend at appropriate points but only exceptionally beyond twenty-one years.

From first forming up at his Regimental depot, the infantry recruit spent some two and a half months on basic training (which included one and a half hours' PT per day) before joining his home battalion. There the annual training cycle pursued its relentless course from section and half-company drills in the spring through to field training at company level, and possibly battalion manoeuvres, in the late summer or early autumn. The modern infantryman may be interested to know that in 1890 the recruits' range course was 200 rounds. The trained soldiers' annual course was also 200 rounds. This was calculated on the basis of 125 rounds fired on range practices and 65 rounds as ordered by the CO for field firing or other exercises, leaving 10 rounds per man for competitions. In addition, the GOC controlled a somewhat modest reserve annual allowance of 1,200 rounds per battalion. Attention was also paid to physical fitness; trained soldiers were required to carry out an annual course involving one hour's PT on alternate days for three months. In addition there was "running drill", beginning at 300 yards and working up to 1,000 yards.

Battalion Transport

On the outbreak of war, certain battalions on the Home Establishment could each expect to be equipped with one forage cart, four small arms ammunition carts and eleven wagons general service (or GS). To draw these, they would be given fifty-eight draught horses, as well as three pack animals (mules) and two riding horses. However, in peacetime, they had to make do with a much smaller scale for training: one forage cart, one wagon GS and five horses. This was authorised by Army Circulars Cl 95 of May 1887 which also noted that the cart and wagon would be marked by Ordnance

2 *Transport section, 1st Bn Oxfordshire Light Infantry 1891 (Army Museums Ogilby Trust)*

before issue "to correspond with the stencilling on the valises, thus –

1 R.F.
Regimental Transport
No 1

Soldiers (24 in war) employed on battalion transport duties were dressed as others except that they wore brown or khaki breeches with blue puttees instead of trousers and leggings (see **Fig 2**). It is intended to illustrate vehicles in a subsequent volume but see the useful contemporary publication *(27)*.

Mounted Infantry

In 1890, the organisation and training at home of mounted infantry was still, in formal terms, at an early stage. An *ad hoc* training unit had been formed at Aldershot in 1888 by Lieutenant Colonel E T H Hutton of the King's Royal Rifle Corps, apparently seconded from a Staff appointment in HQ Aldershot District. His Adjutant was Captain E A J Alderson of the Royal West Kent Regiment, who had already made a name for himself as a mounted infantryman in South Africa (1881) and Egypt (1882), and on the Nile (1884–5). He was to go on to command the troops in Mashonaland during the 1896 rebellion and, later, a mounted infantry unit in the Boer War of 1899. In 1890, the unit in Aldershot was in effect a school and was composed of men drawn from various infantry battalions who were housed and trained together during the winter. There seems to have been no establishment, even for the permanent staff. From a later account *(9)* it appears that horses were provided for the first few years by cavalry Regiments on loan. But Army Estimates for 1890/91 refer to an establishment of 273 horses and eventually the whole unit was put on a more satisfactory footing. Meanwhile, in 1890, officers and men were held on the strength of their own units and wore their own Regimental uniform. Like those employed on battalion transport duties, they wore greyish-brown or khaki breeches and blue puttees instead of trousers and leggings. They are not illustrated by Simkin in this book.

Weapons

Every infantryman with the exception only of the officers, warrant officers and, in some cases, such specialists as the pioneers, was armed with a rifle. In 1889, the new magazine Lee-Metford had begun to be issued so that in 1890 both it and its predecessor, the Martini-Henry, were to be found in service (see **Fig 3**).

The Martini-Henry rifle was a single-shot weapon of .45-inch calibre which fired a hefty 480-grain lead slug. It had a respectable kick and in sustained action tended to become too hot to handle (witness the various accounts of Rorke's Drift). It was 4ft 1½in long, weighed 8lb 10oz and was sighted to 500 yards. Some 70 rounds of ammunition were carried about the person of the soldier and a further 30 rounds were available to him in war in the battalion echelon. The drill for the weapon was laid down in "Field Exercises and Evolutions of the Infantry" published in April 1877. Two bayonets were provided: a triangular socket version was used by junior ranks, while a sword pattern with a wavy blade 18⅜ inches long (see **Fig 3a**) was carried by Sergeants and Colour Sergeants.

The Rifle Magazine Mark I, to give the Lee-Metford its Ordnance nomenclature of 1889, was a great step forward in design and of course it brought with it notable tactical advantages of range and rate of fire. It was our first .303-inch calibre rifle and fired a 215-grain lead bullet. It was, like the

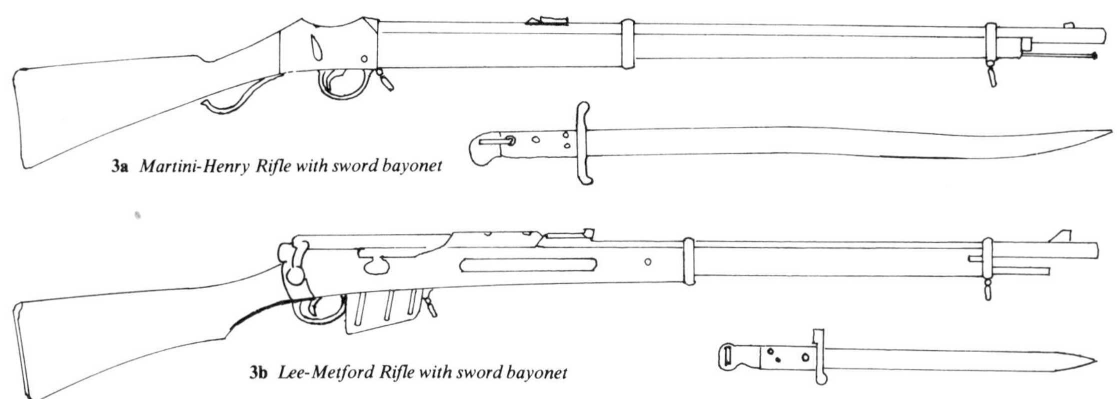

3a *Martini-Henry Rifle with sword bayonet*

3b *Lee-Metford Rifle with sword bayonet*

Martini-Henry, 4ft 1½in long, but was rather heavier at 9lb 8oz. Sighted from 300 yards to 3,500 yards, it was probably most effective out to about 375 yards but was naturally exceedingly accurate, by comparison with the Martini-Henry, to 500 yards and further. Although it was a magazine rifle (provided at first with two magazines of 8 rounds) it was also equipped with a cut-off which, if applied, prevented the bolt from feeding from the magazine. Its contents were thus converted into a reserve and a rifle was once again effectively a single-shot weapon. Nonetheless, mostly because they were much lighter, more rounds were carried: initially a maximum of 90 in the pouches plus 16 in two magazines but eventually 100 in the pouches plus 8 in one magazine. This was backed up in war by a further 85 rounds in the battalion echelon. The drill for the weapon was eventually laid down in "Rifle Exercises 1892" whose publication must, incidentally, have given someone a red face because it is illustrated throughout with drawings of the Martini-Henry! The associated bayonet was the sword variety with a blade 12 inches long for all ranks.

WOs and certain infantry Sergeants carried a Sword Staff Sergeants. The pattern frequently illustrated by Simkin had a slightly curved 32½-inch blade, a gilt guard, and a black leather scabbard with gilt mounts including two loose rings (see **Figs 1** and **4a**). So far as can be determined the same pattern was carried by the Foot Guards, but a slightly different sword and scabbard with guard and mounts of steel was carried by Rifles. Both became obsolescent in 1889 when a new sword (see List of Changes 5629) was introduced. This had a straight 32¾-inch blade and a steel scabbard with two fixed rings (see **Fig 4b**); for WOs and SSgts of Rifles the guard on this sword was steel (soon altered to iron) and for all others it was gilt.

Drummers of Foot Guards and Line carried a drummer's straight "roman" sword (see **Fig 5a**) which had a 13¼-inch blade and a black leather scabbard and was embellished, for

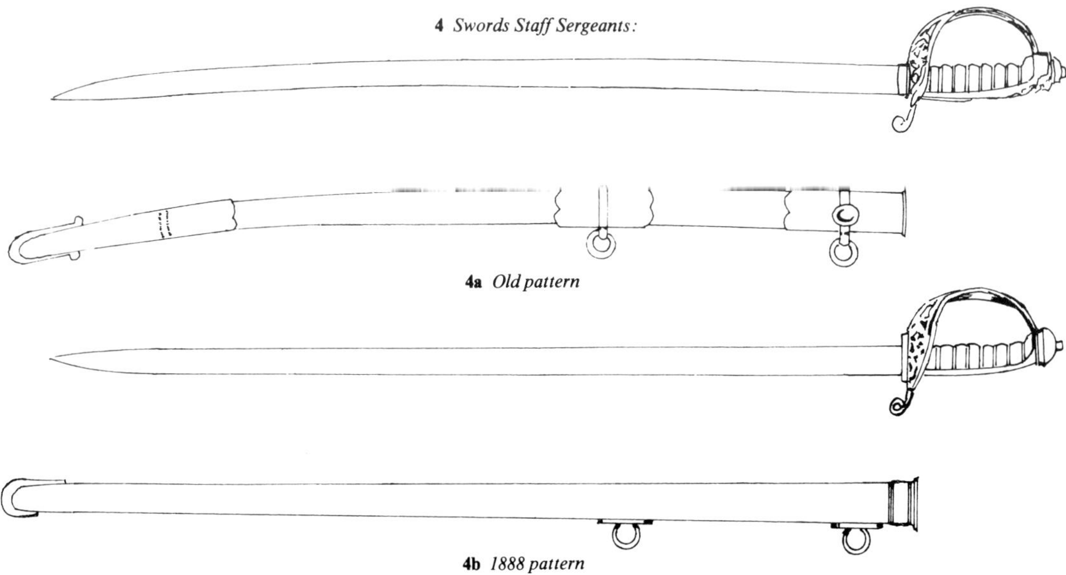

4 *Swords Staff Sergeants:*

4a *Old pattern*

4b *1888 pattern*

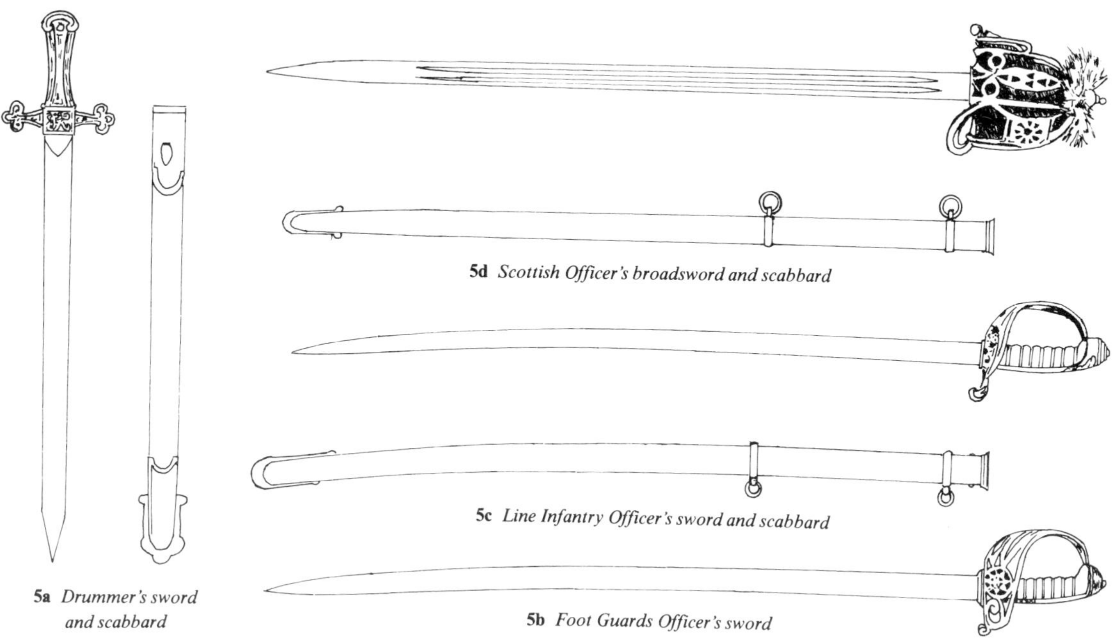

5a Drummer's sword
and scabbard

5d Scottish Officer's broadsword and scabbard

5c Line Infantry Officer's sword and scabbard

5b Foot Guards Officer's sword

Rifles with a steel or iron hilt and mountings and for all others with gilt.

The swords of infantry officers were all in general terms similar. They had a slightly curved blade 32½ inches long, a half-basket hilt and a steel (for junior officers) or brass (for field officers) scabbard with two loose rings. For Foot Guards (**Fig 5b**), the steel guard was pierced with the Regimental emblem; for Line infantry (**Fig 5c**) the guard was gilt and was pierced with the royal cypher "VR"; for Rifles the guard was steel and was pierced with a crown and stringed bugle-horn.

Officers of Scottish Regiments (except the Scottish Rifles) carried a broadsword or claymore (**Fig 5d**) with a straight 32-inch blade; for most Regiments it had a steel basket hilt lined with red cloth and a steel scabbard with two loose rings. But on active service and in certain orders of dress at home, the basket hilt was exchanged in several Regiments for a cross-hilt (see **Fig 79**) carried by junior officers or a half-basket hilt carried by field officers (see **Fig 84**). There is unfortunately not space to go into all the varieties of the Scottish sword which may have been worn in 1890, nor can we do more than take a cursory glance in the Regimental sections further on at such weaponry as skean dhu or dirks. Information on all edged weapons together with excellent photographs is to be found in Robert Wilkinson-Latham's book *(21)* on the subject.

Finally WOs and certain other appointments were provided in war with a pistol while officers were required to provide themselves with one which would accept service ammunition. The situation here was just as in the cavalry – see page 15 of Volume I.

Uniform and Personal Equipment

Although from nearly every other point of view, one battalion of infantry was much like another, uniform varied enormously. For this reason, the coloured plates of infantry and the accompanying text which follow have been divided into groups for: (a) Foot Guards, (b) English, Welsh and Irish Line, (c) Scottish Line, and (d) Rifles. As in Volume I a general description of the dress of each group is followed, Regiment by Regiment, with a more detailed account related to the figures in the coloured plates and the photographs. This means that the treatment of each Regiment is not the same but unfortunately this is forced upon us by lack of space. However, while dress was often very different, personal equipment was generally more uniform though then, as now, there were interesting exceptions – as we shall see. Items of equipment issued to infantry soldiers (and to those of most dismounted arms) in 1890 began with "Valise Equipment". The pattern 1882 was obsolescent but still in use with many units either because they were awaiting issue of the pattern 1888, or because they were deliberately retaining it so long as they had the Martini-Henry rifle; the 1882 pattern pouches were suitable for that ammunition while the manufacture of pattern 1888 was very quickly (June 1890 – List of Changes 6105) concentrated on pouches suitable only for .303-inch rounds. Variations in unit practice are well illustrated further on in the book. The items of equipment were:

Valise Equipment 1882: (See **Fig 6**). The waistbelt was adjustable at either end and had two brass loops in the centre of the back which could be pushed down when not needed; the clasp or locket was brass and of the type illustrated except for Rifles who had a yellow metal "snake" clasp. The ammunition

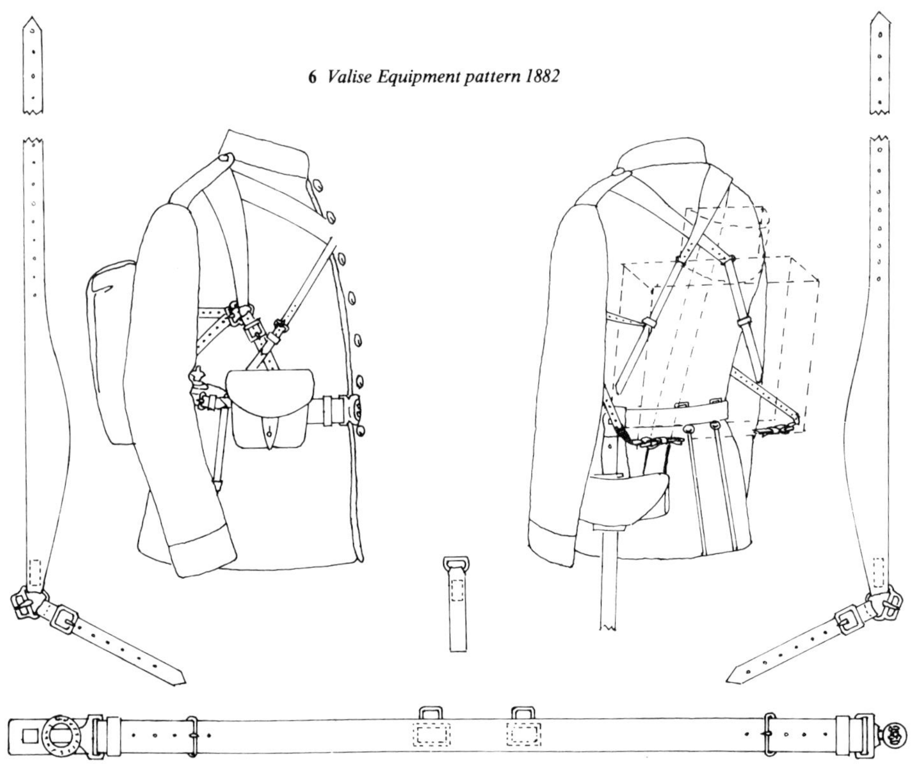

pouches had two leather loops at the back and slipped onto the belt; at the top rear of each pouch was a brass loop to which the brace, if worn, was secured. The braces, right and left, were issued as illustrated with the two component straps already sewn to the connecting three-way buckle or "ring". For those units which wore only one pouch (Medical Staff Corps, Ordnance Store Corps, etc) there was a simple chape (or brace attachment) made with a loop so that it could be slipped over the waistbelt and at the top a brass "D" to which the brace was attached, the valise itself was 15 inches wide by 11½ inches deep and its flap was secured over the contents with two straps and buckles which fastened at the back; on the "front" of the valise (i.e. the side up against the soldier's back) two white straps were secured at an angle to the vertical with a buckle at the upper end and a fixed loop halfway down. To attach the valise to the remainder of the equipment, the belt was first fitted with the pouches and put on; the braces were then put over the shoulders and the lower strap passed through the brass "D" or loop on the top of each pouch from the rear, brought up, buckled and then pushed through the ring and down again between the brace and the tunic; the long part of the brace went over the shoulders and crossed over before being passed through the valise buckle; this was adjusted to bring the top of the valise in line with the armpits; the brace was then passed through the fixed loop on the valise; it was next taken forward under the arm to the "ring" where it was again buckled before finally passing back to be buckled on the

underside of the valise. From this, it will be appreciated that soldiers were only being reasonable when they complained that the braces cut them under the arms, and that the valise could not very easily be taken off without shedding everything else as well! There was one other problem and that was that when the soldier did anything strenuous having forgotten or been unable to secure his pouch first, or when he simply lay down to shoot and opened his pouch to get out a round, his ammunition tended to fall out; this problem was not at first cured by the next set of equipment, but the other two sources of complaint were effectively removed by what became known as the "Slade-Wallace" equipment.

Valise Equipment Pattern 1888: (See **Fig 7**). This design was sold to the Government by Colonels Slade and Wallace, after whom it eventually became known. Once again the waist-belt was adjustable at either end but it now had brace attach-ments (or brass rings attached to running loops) on the belt and there were three buckles on the back. (To economise on buff leather the belt later came to be made in two or three pieces, rather than one). The pouches had special fittings inside and outside to enable at first 40 rounds to be carried on the right and 50 on the left and then eventually 50 on each side. To assemble the equipment, the pouches, which had loops on the back, were slipped onto the waistbelt with the running loop (or brace attachment of the belt) so adjusted as to be in the centre of each pouch. The braces, each of two straps joined by a double-ended buckle, were put over the shoulders and the

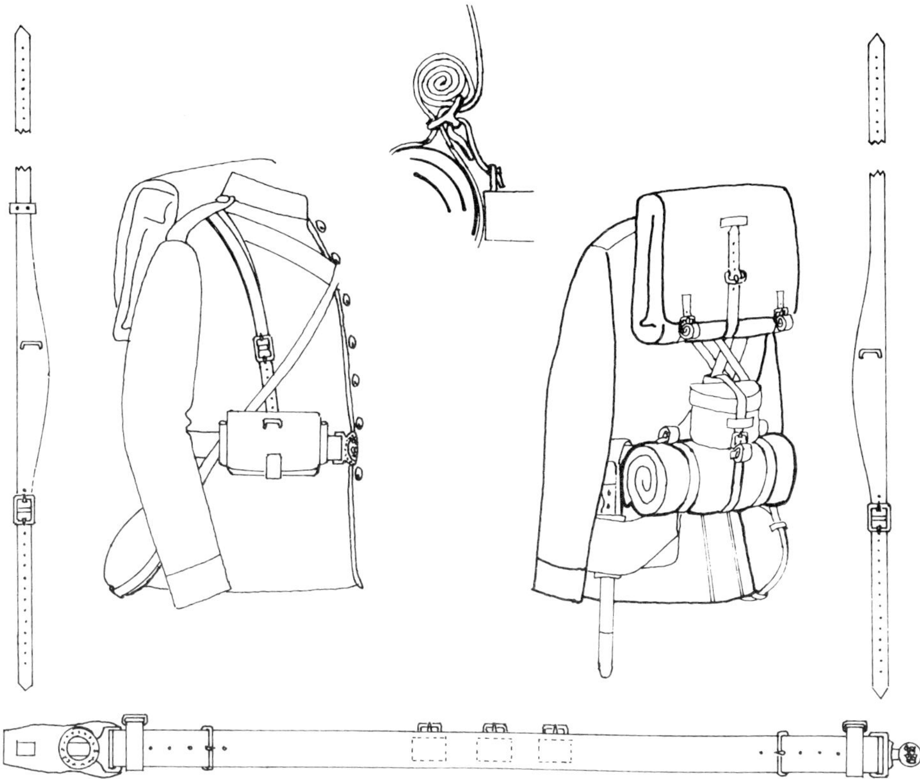

7 Valise Equipment pattern 1888 (Inset: The chape or tab attaching the brace and rolled greatcoat to the waistbelt.)

shorter strap attached behind the pouch in much the same way as with the 1882 pattern equipment; behind, the long straps were crossed through a runner and then each was passed through a buckle attached to a short chape or tab; the tabs were attached to the outer two buckles on the back of the waistbelt; the braces, being much longer (at 5ft 10¾in) than the 1882 pattern, had still enough length to be passed around the rolled greatcoat and buckled back onto the chape or tab; the remaining length of each brace was then rolled to that buckle. The valise which was smaller than its predecessor (at 15in wide by 7½in deep) was attached by two white straps; these were permanently fastened to the back of the valise and were passed forwards over each shoulder through the brass "D" on the wide part of the brace and down to the upper part of the double buckle where they were secured.

All items of both equipment were of white buff with brass fittings (or black leather with yellow metal fittings for Rifles) except for the valises which were of black japanned canvas. With either of them the following additional items of equipment were worn in 1890:

Haversack: (See **Fig 8a**). Made of white canvas with a brass buckle on the strap, or of black canvas with black japanned (or enamelled) buckle for Rifles, the haversack measured about 12 inches across by 8¾ inches deep. It was always put on first, with the strap over the right shoulder. When not required (to carry the day's rations, or anything else) the haversack was generally

rolled up and positioned to hang outside the bayonet scabbard; it was ordered (QRs 1889 Section XII sub-paragraph 42d) that the top of the haversack should be "in line with the top of the scabbard, but not above it."

Water-bottle: Two patterns were in use at this time: the so-called Italian pattern (**Fig 8b**) was just over 6 inches tall, was made of wood and bound with iron straps at the top and bottom; it was secured in a white buff carriage with its strap over the left shoulder. (The same water-bottle had originally been attached to the 1882 equipment by means of a spring clip on to the waistbelt; this system was abandoned from 1885). The new "bottle water enamelled" was approved in 1888 and began to be issued in 1889 or 1890; it was round (see **Fig 8c**) and was covered with gray felt; the carriage was a white buff strap which was passed through metal loops on the side and bottom of the water-bottle and slung over the left shoulder. The water-bottle was always put on last.

Bayonet Frog: There were essentially two patterns in use; a plain frog (see **Fig 8d**) for use by infantry R&F and one incorporating a strap and buckle across the front (see **Fig 8e**) for other dismounted men armed with sword-bayonets. The former type was 9¼ inches long and the latter varied up to 10½ inches for the longest pattern (for RA and RE).

Mess-tin and Cover: The mess-tin was a semi-circular metal affair carried in a black japanned canvas case. With the 1882 equipment, it was secured by a single white buff strap to

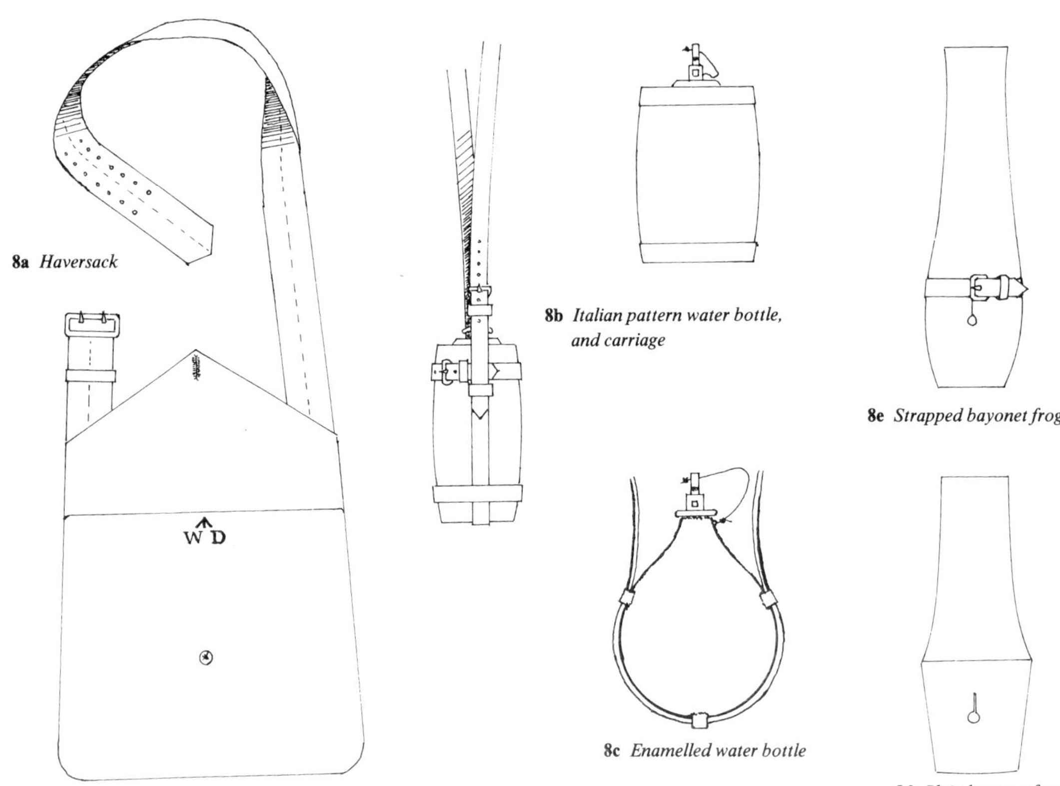

the top of the valise (see **Fig 1**). With the 1888 pattern, it was secured on top of the rolled greatcoat by a single white buff strap which was passed through the runner connecting the braces where they crossed at the back.

Spare Magazine Pouch: When the Rifle Magazine Mk I was first issued, it was accompanied by a second magazine and a small leather pouch in which to carry it. It was of black leather for Rifles and white buff for others; when ordered, it was slipped over the left brace above the ammunition pouch (see **Fig 21**). (Note, however, that it was ordered to be withdrawn in Feb 1891, within two years of first being issued.)

Intrenching Implement: This was introduced into service in 1882 but there was evidently some difficulty in deciding how the unfortunate infantryman was to carry it; the original item (List of Changes 4153) says, enigmatically "With each implement of this description ... two straps have been supplied for use in carrying it according to special instructions which have been given on that point ... This arrangement is subject to modification after experience ..." What these instructions said has not been determined but in the end a frog (black for Rifles; white for others) was designed to be worn on the waistbelt next to and overlapping the bayonet frog. It and the implement itself are illustrated at **Fig 9**. From this it is clear that the bayonet would hang to the rear of the implement, being passed through the loop marked "B", on the frog. Not shown is an additional black leather strap which was provided

loose and was intended to be stitched to the implement handle by Regimental tradesmen and then used to buckle the bayonet scabbard tightly to the implement. Photographs of the implement being used seem to be rare and this is no doubt due to the unpopularity of the tool, then as now. A good digging implement has to be big enough to "heft" and heavy enough to make some impression on difficult soil, let alone rocks and roots; but then it is impossible to hitch such an article to an infantryman's kit without all but immobilising him. Inevitably perhaps the result over the last hundred years seems to have been a design victory for convenience and lightness in carrying, over weight and general effectiveness as an implement. Unpopular kit is seldom used.

Leggings. Made of black leather, these were about 9 inches in height and were fastened down the outside of the ankle by a lace passed through four eyelets. The lace was tied under a black leather strap which went all round the top of the legging, secured by a small brass buckle.

From 1886, valise equipment ceased to be issued to, or worn by, WOs of infantry and dismounted arms. Some Sergeants were also freed of the burden and these included the following infantry battalion appointments: Quartermaster Sergeant, Orderly Room Sergeant, Sergeant Instructor of Musketry, Band Sergeant, Sergeant Drummer, Sergeant Bugler (Light Infantry and Rifles only), and Sergeant Piper (Scottish Regiments only). All these except the Piper wore a plain waistbelt

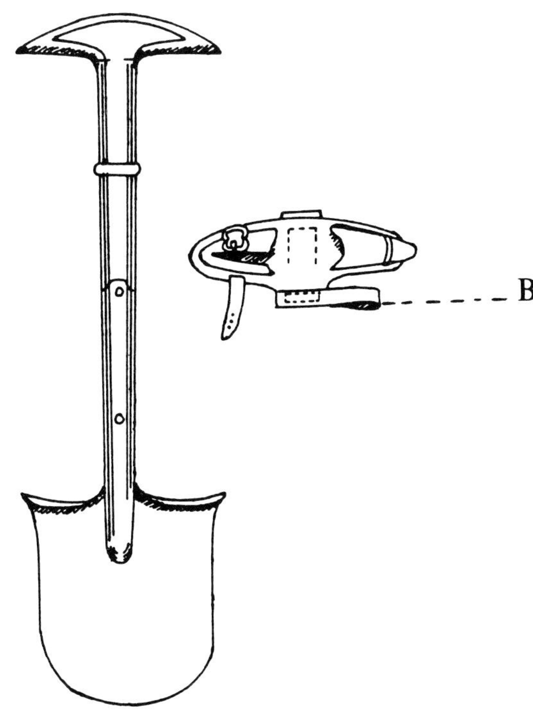

9 *Intrenching implement and frog*

or more usually, a sword belt of black leather for Rifles or of white enamelled leather for others. There were certain differences between Foot Guards and Line which will be described later but in general the sword belt was of two pieces of leather joined by a metal ring under the left arm; to this ring was attached a sword hook and the short carriage 13¾ inches long; the long carriage (31in) had a loop at the top and slid along the belt; finally there was an adjusting buckle on the wearer's right side of the belt.

Officers' sword belts will be described later on in the notes accompanying Regiments or groups of Regiments.

The Drums

The establishment of a battalion provided for a Sergeant Drummer and sixteen drummers in Guards and Line Infantry, or a Sergeant Bugler and sixteen buglers in Light Infantry and Rifles. Highland battalions, had in addition, a Sergeant Piper and a number of pipers some officially allowed and some unofficially (mis)employed men; the total was often double the size of the normal Corps of Drums. Drummers were required also to be buglers and had originally been introduced by way of a fore-runner to radio as a means of communication between the Company Commander and his men. At first, therefore, it was less common to "brigade" them under the Drum (or Bugle)

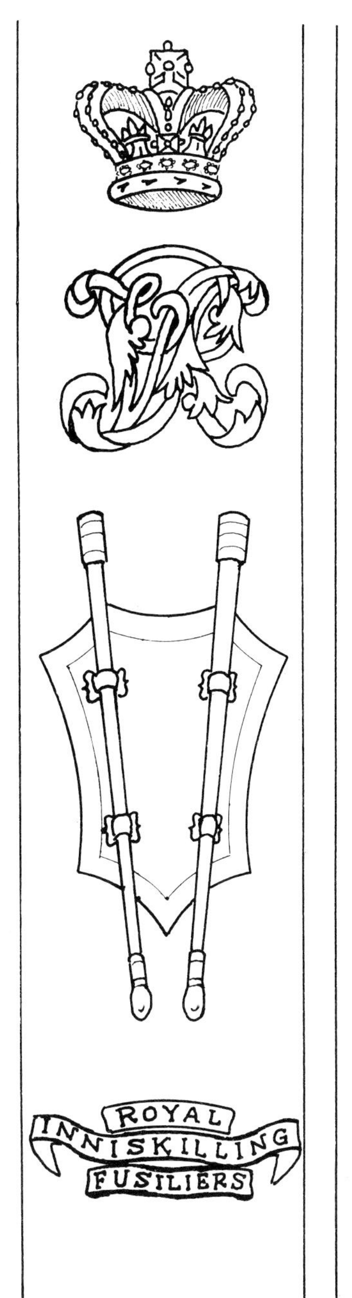

10 *Sergeant Drummer's belt*

Major – who in 1881 was down-graded from Staff Sergeant to Sergeant and re-styled the Sergeant Drummer (or Bugler). By 1890, however, while companies still needed and had their two drummers, it was increasingly common to see them all formed up together as a corps. Between the sixteen, on such occasions, one might have expected to see six side-drummers, a bass drummer, a cymballist and eight flutes (including perhaps one piccolo); but this was not laid down and examination of old photographs will produce a variety of arrangements. The Drums, it is interesting to note, were (and remain today) under the direct supervision of the Adjutant of the Battalion and have nothing to do with the Band.

The Sergeant Drummer

Although downgraded to Sergeant in rank, the Sergeant Drummer continued to be dressed basically as a Staff Sergeant. This entitled him to a tunic of first class quality with certain embellishments and to these more were added by virtue of his particular appointment; all this will be described in more detail further on in the book. But besides his coat the Sergeant Drummer (but not the Sergeant Bugler) had two other special items or "appointments"; these were his staff (often now called a mace) and his shoulder belt. These were issued to all except Light Infantry and Rifle battalions and were of the following designs:

Staff: Measuring 5ft 2in overall, it was made of malacca cane and fitted with a round gilt top, a gilt collar and chains and a gilt ferrule. The top was surmounted by a crown; around the centre and lower parts were gilt or silvered badges or devices and scrolls; at the base of the round top there was a standard design of foliage. The details of staves carried by various Regiments are described elsewhere in the relevant section including several cases in which Regiments provided their Sergeant Drummer with a non-regulation staff of special design.

Belt: There were two types in use: the Ordnance issue belt (see **Fig 10**) was made of cloth of the facing colour of the Regiment. It was plainly embellished with a double line of gold lace down each edge. On the front in the centre of the chest was the Royal Cypher crowned, embroidered in gold, silver and colours, over a silvered shield bearing two miniature silver-mounted ebony drumsticks. Below that the title of the Regiment was embroidered in gold on a label of the facing colour, itself edged with gold. The Foot Guards, however, received belts which were more richly embellished with badges and battle honours covering most of the front. This type was adopted by some Line Regiments at their own expense and in preference to the Ordnance issue belt. Some examples are to be seen elsewhere in the book.

The Drummer

All the sixteen drummers were trained to play the side drum and the bugle; some or all would also play the other instruments. All were dressed the same and ranked between Private and Corporal. Embellishments on the tunic varied between Guards and Line, and are described elsewhere. Equipment carried by all included a sword (see **Fig 5a** and page 18) and a bugle (see **Fig 1**), which was made of copper and mounted with brass fittings. The bugle was suspended from the left shoulder to hang behind the right hip by a cord which was usually red, blue and yellow for Royal (including Foot Guards) Regiments and green for others. Flute-players (or, more correctly, flautists) may have had a white buff case on the front of the waistbelt while bass-drummers wore an apron (usually of scarlet) and the special carriage for their equipment; neither of these is illustrated in this book and there is therefore no further description. Side-drummers wore the appropriate carriage over the right shoulder and, in some Regiments, wore a white apron on the left leg in order to protect the trousers from wear. The side-drum in 1890 consisted of a brass case with wooden hoops 2 inches deep; the heads were of calfskin; the rope tensioner was of white hemp passed through eight white buff braces; the plaited drag ropes were also white hemp and were intended to hang 6 inches from the ground. The brass case was often painted on the forward side in the facing colour of the Regiment and embellished with the appropriate title, badges and battle honours.

Marking of Equipment

Equipment Regulations 1881 Section XVI provided for the marking of nearly everything a soldier used from a wagon to a water-bottle. Personal items such as clothing were marked with his name and number. Unit items, which then as now included his equipment, were generally marked with the unit title and a company serial number. For example an Italian pattern water-bottle might have been stamped on the top, near the lip, "1 SG 813" indicating that it was water-bottle No 813 on charge to 1st Bn Scots Guards. But this was very small and the only marking on personal equipment readily visible to the observer was the Regimental title painted on the back of the valise by Line infantry (Foot Guards were identified by a metal Regimental valise star described elsewhere). Precluded by Equipment Regulations 1881, this particular marking was introduced by Army Circulars Cl 46 of Feb 1888. Titles for infantry were not specified but photographs (for example, **Fig 48**) show that an abbreviated form was used. This was usually the same as that employed on the men's shoulder-straps with the battalion number shown in front. Markings were made in white paint using (probably) $1\frac{1}{2}$-inch stencils.

Mounted Officers

The Commanding Officer, two Majors (known for parade purposes as the "right major" and the "left major") and the Adjutant were mounted. The dress of these officers, when on mounted duties, included knee boots and spurs, and a sabretache attached to the sword belt. Horse furniture – (see pages 17 and 18 of Volume I for an explanation of the terms) consisted of: on the horse's head, head collar and bridle of brown leather with gilt bit bosses, and a front or browband and rosettes in the Regimental facing colour, steel chain rein and brown leather reins; brown leather saddle secured with a blue webbing girth; brown leather wallets with black bearskin covers; brown leather breast plate with gilt boss, steel bit and stirrups.

Orders of Dress

Orders of Dress were laid down for officers and men separately in Queen's Regulations and the following has been extracted from QRs 1889 and from AOs of 1890. Excluding Mess Dress which is neither illustrated nor described in this book, there were four basic orders of dress:

Review Order: (To be worn in the presence of the Sovereign, for Royal escorts and guards of honour, at all state ceremonies, and otherwise when specially ordered.) Full dress headdress, tunic or doublet, trousers or kilt; waistbelt and sash according to rank; when ammunition was not carried, a single pouch to be worn by Other Ranks on the waistbelt in the centre of the back; haversacks, water-bottles and leggings to be worn only if specially ordered.

Marching Order: (To be worn on the line of march, at route-marching, in the field for inspection by General Officers, and on other occasions when specially ordered. In subsidiary paragraphs it is noted, however, that infantry were as a general rule to turn out for their usual daily parade in marching order.) For Officers: the full dress headdress; tunic (or doublet), except that the light cloth or serge second tunic (see Dress Regulations 1883: apart from the material of the garment itself, the same as the dress tunic) was permitted in lieu; trousers or kilt, waistbelt and sash according to rank; boots and leggings. For Other Ranks: full dress headdress; frock; complete kit and equipment (i.e. the complete valise equipment with contents as detailed in standing orders, the haversack, water-bottle, leggings, waterproof sheet, cape and greatcoat); spade and reserve magazine pouch only when ordered.

Field Day Order: (To be worn for summer field days, divisional and brigade drills – which refers not to ceremonial drills but to tactical or manoeuvre drills – and by individuals employed on certain duties, such as garrison orderlies.) For Officers: the same as Marching Order. For Other Ranks: as for Marching Order but without the following unless specially ordered; valise (therefore also its contents), cape and greatcoat, haversack, water-bottle and leggings. From contemporary photographs, it would seem that the last three usually were "specially ordered"!

Drill Order: (To be worn for ordinary drills or in other words for training in barracks.) For Officers: undress headdress, patrol jacket and trousers; sash and waistbelt. For Other Ranks: forage cap, frock and trousers; belt with right pouch in the centre of the back unless the mess-tin or ammunition was carried, when the pouch was to be worn in front on the right; leggings, haversack and water-bottle only when specially ordered.

FOOT GUARDS

General Introduction

In his "Social Life in the British Army" *(1)* published in 1900, "A British Officer" remarked: "There appears to be a general impression among civilians not well acquainted with Her Majesty's Guards that their military duties are light and chiefly ornamental. This is very far from being the case. It is doubtful if keener soldiers are to be found in any branch of the service; in the minutiae of drill the greatest accuracy is insisted on, and the study of the higher branches of the profession of arms is encouraged in every possible manner." Of course, by the standards of today, drill was immensely important. Far more was done as a drill with parade-ground precision then than now, though the term is still in common enough use. Foot- and arms-drill, and evolutions on the square, are the ceremonial legacies of the precise and studied evolutions which our infantry predecessors of the eighteenth century, and to a lesser extent, the Napoleonic era, performed in order to give battle. Despite the exhortation of Lord Wolseley (see page 15) in his introduction to Infantry Drill 1889, the training of the infantry in the 1890s had much more in common with 1814 than 1914. And yet in 1890 by all the contemporary standards by which infantry may be judged, the Warrant Officers, Sergeants and rank and file of the Foot Guards were very good indeed. As to the officers and their study of the "higher branches of the profession" it is worth noting that of sixty-four students at the Staff College in 1890, three of the forty-two infantry officers were guardsmen. This is a ratio of 1 : 14 and may be favourably compared with the 1 : 21 ratio of Guards to infantry battalions at large. In two important respects, therefore, the Foot Guards were setting an example to the rest of the infantry. What then did they look like?

Other Ranks' Full Dress

As with nearly every other branch of the service in 1890, the Foot Guards had all but reached the final development of their full dress uniform. Its general form is well known today and photographs both in colour and monochrome are readily available. And yet their uniforms are full of little pitfalls for the unwary. Some details have changed since 1890 and the reader is advised not to make assumptions concerning items of dress not described in this book whether for 1980 or 1890. At that time, the guardsman was not yet called a Guardsman but a Private, and his dress uniform was as follows (see **Figs 11** and **12**).

The black bearskin was common to all Regiments, together with its brass curb-chain; plumes were peculiar to the two senior Regiments. The scarlet tunic had a blue collar cut low, rounded in front and piped on the front and top in white; the shoulder straps were blue piped white along the sides and round the top; the cuffs were blue, edged with white piping and superimposed on the front was a blue slash or flap edged white on the top, rear and bottom edges; there was white piping down the chest and down the centre of the rear skirts; false pockets on the skirts behind were of scarlet, piped on the inner edge and horizontally with dark blue; badges on the collar and shoulder straps, and worsted loops on the cuff slashes and skirts were of Regimental design; finally, buttons were grouped according to Regimental seniority. The trousers were dark blue with narrow scarlet welts and boots were black.

In general terms, this dress was also worn by NCOs of the Foot Guards. However, there were three classes of tunic, not to mention a variety of embellishments and badges, and these are listed below on the basis of contemporary evidence and the work of Maj Dawnay *(6)*. The reader should, however, note that the tunics of drummers (and musicians who are not shown in this book) were different, and that pipers of the Scots Guards wore a blue doublet. Badges of rank and appointment shown in the lists below were worn with one exception (which is detailed) on the right arm, above the elbow; all chevrons were worn point downwards.

Rank and File Class Tunic

This was as described above with Regimental badges on the collar and shoulder straps embroidered in white; loops of white worsted on the cuff slashes and on the skirts; brass

11 *Privates 1st Bn Grenadier Guards circa 1893 (Army Museums Ogilby Trust)*

Regimental buttons on the cuffs but not on the skirts. The rank and file tunic was worn by:

Rank	Appointment	Badge
Private	—	None.
Private	Pioneer	Crossed axes with Regimental badge (GG – Grenade; CG – rose; SG – star) in white on a blue ground.
Private Corporal	Lance Corporal } —	Two chevrons of white worsted, edged blue on a scarlet ground (see **Fig 23b**) which although a drummer's tunic, illustrates the make up of chevrons – the second having been removed for this purpose).
Corporal	Lance Sergeant	Three chevrons of white worsted edged blue, on a scarlet ground (see **Fig 12**).

Good conduct badges (chevrons, point uppermost) were of white worsted edged blue on a scarlet ground and were worn on the left forearm; these badges were of "single" width, or about half that of chevrons of rank. Qualification badges were also worn on the left forearm above any good conduct badge, and were of worsted embroidery (usually white) on a blue ground.

Sergeants' Class Tunic

This tunic was as described above but with Regimental badges on the collar and shoulder straps embroidered in gold or silver wire, and the loops on the cuff slashes and skirts were of gold lace. The tunic was worn by:

Rank	Appointment	Badges and Embellishments
Sergeant	—	Three gold lace chevrons edged blue on a scarlet ground.
Sergeant	Pioneer	Three gold lace chevrons as above with, above, crossed axes embroidered in gold, and Regimental badge (as above for Pioneer Privates) embroidered in silver, both on a blue ground.
Sergeant	Assistant Instructor of Signalling	Three gold lace chevrons as above, with, above crossed signalling flags embroidered in gold on a blue ground.
Colour Sergeant	—	Three gold lace chevrons edged blue on a scarlet ground with Colour badge of Regimental design superimposed.
Sergeant	Orderly Room Clerk	As above for Sergeant.*
Staff Sergeant	Orderly Room Clerk	As above for Colour Sergeant.*
Quartermaster Sergeant	Orderly Room Clerk	Four gold lace chevrons edged blue on a scarlet ground.*
Staff Sergeant	Assistant Orderly Room Clerk	As above for Sergeant Orderly Room Clerk.*

*(Note 1) Tunic laced in addition as 1st Class but with only one row of gold lace round cuff.

Rank	Appointment	Badges and Embellishments
Staff Sergeant	Assistant Regimental Clerk	As above for Sergeant Orderly Room Clerk.
Staff Sergeant	Battalion Drill Sergeant	Three gold lace chevrons edged blue on a scarlet ground with Colour badge superimposed.†
Staff Sergeant	Sergeant Instructor of Musketry	Three gold lace chevrons edged blue on a scarlet ground with, above, a crown over crossed rifles in gold, etc on scarlet.†

†Tunic laced in addition as 1st Class.

Good conduct badges were not worn by Sergeants and above. Qualification badges were embroidered in gold/silver on a blue ground.

12 *Lance Sergeants Coldstream (left) and Scots (right) Guards circa 1892 (George Bush Collection)*

1st Class Tunic

This tunic was basically the same as Sergeants' quality but had in addition: gold lace around the top and front of the collar, inside the white piping; a gold lace patch on either side of the collar extending from the front to the shoulder strap button with, on it, the Regimental badge embroidered in silver on a blue ground; shoulder straps edged with narrow gold braid (instead of white piping); round the cuff a double row of gold lace below the white piping; on the cuff slash, gold lace inside (and just sufficiently separated to show a blue light) the white piping on the top, rear and bottom; similar gold lace on the rear skirts, and Regimental buttons on the lace loops. The tunic was worn by:

Rank	Appointment	Badge
Quartermaster Sergeant	Regimental Quartermaster Sergeant	Four gold lace chevrons edged blue on scarlet ground with, above, an eight-point star embroidered in gold on a blue ground.
Warrant Officer	Superintending Clerk	A crown embroidered in gold, silver and colours on a blue ground (worn on the right forearm – Note 2).
Warrant Officer	Sergeant Major	The large-size Royal Arms embroidered in gold, silver and colours on a scarlet ground (Note 3).

13 *Sergeant Major Coldstream Guards circa 1890*

Notes:

1. Although what is shown here for an Orderly Room Clerk ranking as Sergeant reflects the regulations, it amounts to the dress of a Staff Sergeant. It also seems odd that there should have been no distinction of dress between this appointment and those of Assistant Regimental Clerk and Assistant Orderly-Room Clerk. More research is needed.

2. The author has yet to locate a photograph showing this badge being worn – though **Fig 13** may be an example.

3. The large Royal Arms badge had been worn for some years superimposed upon four gold lace chevrons. The regulation was changed in 1882 and the Royal Arms would appear to have been removed by about 1885 in favour of a crown, as for the Superintending Clerk. This was probably a fairly unpopular move and the large Royal Arms badge was restored (but this time on its own) in 1890 or 1891.

Other Dress Distinctions

Besides wearing tunics of different qualities, WOs and NCOs exhibited certain other differences in full dress. Sergeants (i.e. full Sergeants but not Lance Sergeants) and above wore a cut feather plume in the bearskin. They also wore a crimson sash over the right shoulder which was intended to meet just behind the left hip; it was secured by a loop of the same material below which cord tassels fell to the bottom of the tunic skirts. Since about 1887 (see Army Circulars Cl 115 of 1886 and Cl 152 of Sep 1887) valise equipment was not issued to the following appointments: Sergeant Major, Bandmaster, Superintending Clerk, Quartermaster Sergeant, Orderly Room Sergeants, Band Sergeants and Sergeant Drummers (also Sergeant Pipers). Although not mentioned, the order evidently applied to that peculiarity of the Foot Guards, the Drill Sergeants as well. All these appointments wore a Sword Staff Sergeant (see page 18 and **Fig 4**) with a sword knot composed of a gold strap and acorn. The sword belt was of white enamelled leather 1½ inches wide and fitted with a round gilt locket of Regimental design; a buckle for adjusting the length was incorporated on the wearer's right; the sword was suspended by short and long white enamelled leather carriages; all fittings, including the hook positioned on the belt forward of the short carriage, were of yellow metal.

Drummers

Drummers ranked from Private to Corporal and wore the rank and file tunic of their Regiment. This was embellished with drummer's lace – white with blue fleurs-de-lys – in three widths, as follows (see **Fig 23a** and **b** for a Coldstream Guards example): ½-inch lace on the top front and bottom of the collar; a blue and white fringe below the top line of lace covered the remainder of the collar; ½-inch lace around the shoulder straps, and on the inner edge of the wings which were blue; ⅝-inch lace doubled in loops across the chest; finally, ¾-inch lace on the seams of the sleeves and the back, across and on the outer edge of the wings, and forming inverted chevrons on each sleeve; the lace loops on the cuff slashes were of ⅝-inch lace and those of the tails were of ¾-inch lace; the latter were edged with blue piping for privates and were without buttons. Side drums were painted blue and were emblazoned in full colour with the Royal Coat of Arms and Regimental distinctions; the hoops varied in colour but all other accessories including the blue and white striped cotton case (or cover) were standard. The drummer's sword was as illustrated in **Fig 5a** and had a brass hilt and a black scabbard with brass fittings. A drummer usually wore an apron which was of white buff, it was attached to his waistbelt and secured behind the left knee with three narrow white buff straps and buckles. Finally, one other characteristic of the dress of Foot Guards drummers was that good conduct badges were worn upside down (i.e. point downwards) in order to distinguish them from the chevrons of drummer's lace on the sleeve.

Sergeant-Drummers

On great occasions, the Sergeant Drummers of Foot Guards together with all members of the Household Cavalry Regimental Bands wore State dress. This is not described in this book. In full dress, the 1st class tunic was worn but with gold lace on the seams and sleeves in much the same manner as drummers, see **Fig 14**; a difference, however, lay in the fact that there were nine (rather than seven) chevrons of lace on the sleeves, including the double one at the cuff. The Sergeant Drummer's badge was a four-bar chevron of gold lace on blue ground worn point upwards on the forearm. Although a Sergeant, he was dressed and accounted as a Staff Sergeant – see page 18 for details of sword and sword belt. The Sergeant Drummer also wore a crimson sash over his right shoulder and a belt or sash of Regimental design (but of Ordnance provision) over his left shoulder. In addition, of course, he carried a gilt and silver embellished staff of malacca cane.

14 Sergeant Major and Sergeants 1st Bn Coldstream Guards circa 1898

Other Ranks' Undress

This is not shown by Simkin in the present collection of watercolours, but does appear in **Figs 15** and **17**. Soldiers up to the rank of Colour Sergeant wore a short white serge jacket for drill. More senior NCOs had an undress scarlet tunic which was distinguished by a total absence of badges of rank and an almost total absence of gold braid. The white jacket (see **Fig 17**) was perfectly plain with white cord shoulder straps, eight small Regimental buttons down the front, one on each shoulder cord and one on each cuff. Badges of rank on the right upper arm and good conduct badges on the left forearm were of white worsted edged blue on a scarlet ground. As with jackets, so with headdress: Sergeants and below wore a round "pill-box" cap of Regimental pattern secured, usually over the right ear, by a narrow patent leather chinstrap. More senior NCOs wore a round forage cap (see **Figs 13** and **14**) with a gold lace band and a sharply drooping black patent leather peak. The latter was edged with gold lace which varied in width by rank. Each Regiment displayed its badge (or "cap star" as it is known in the Scots Guards) on these caps. There was no special embellishment on either the white jacket or the pill-box cap of drummers.

Officers' Full Dress

Junior officers wore a bearskin which in 1890 seems to have been the same size and shape as those of the men, though before the end of the century it was to become taller and more as we know it today. The tunic was cut in the same style as the men but the collar had a line of gold lace all round the top inside the white piping, and a gold lace "patch" at either end which reached to almost the shoulder strap button; on it was embroidered the Regimental collar badge; the cuffs had a line of gold lace below the white piping and the cuff slashes, whose shape was more stylised than those of the men, had gold lace loops upon which gilt buttons were mounted; the shoulder straps were blue and were edged on the sides and round the top with a double line of narrow gold lace: the scarlet tail slashes were edged with white piping inside and along the bottom, and the gilt buttons were mounted (as on the cuff slashes) on gold lace loops; there was a single line of white piping between the skirt slashes, and a gilt button at the top of each slash: all gold lace was "purl", or scalloped along the edge. The trousers were blue with 2-inch scarlet stripes. A crimson silk sash was worn over the left shoulder and knotted behind the right hip with tassels falling to the level of the tunic skirt. An enamelled white leather sword belt with circular gilt clasp of Regimental design supported the sword hook and sword slings. The sword was as described on page 19 and the knot was of gold cord with a gold acorn. White gloves were worn.

On State occasions and in the presence of the Queen, officers wore a gold and crimson sash, and a gold lace sword belt with gold lace slings on crimson morocco leather, in place of the articles described above. They also wore trousers with gold lace, instead of scarlet, stripes at levees, drawing rooms and in the evenings.

15 *Drill Sergeant Grenadier Guards with Privates of Grenadier, Coldstream and Scots Guards circa 1897*

Officers' Undress

In drill order, officers wore the undress round peaked cap, the sash over a very dark blue almost black frockcoat embellished with black mohair braid, white sword belt and sword, and full dress trousers with scarlet stripes over black boots. This dress is not specially illustrated and described in this book. However, apart from the cap which has changed shape and the sash which has moved from the shoulder to the waist, it has remained very much the same since 1890. It may sometimes be seen today in wear by the Adjutant of a Foot Guards battalion on Public Duties in London.

Valise Star

Unlike Line Regiments whose valises were stencilled with the abbreviated battalion title in white paint, Foot Guards identified theirs with a yellow metal plate. This was of Regimental design and was fastened in the centre of the valise by a strap passed through two loops on the back of the plate.

The Grenadier Guards

Titles:

1660–1685	The King's Royal Regiment of Guards
1685–1815	The First Regiment of Foot Guards
1815–	Grenadier Guards

Badges:

The Royal Cypher and Crown.
A Grenade. Authorised in 1815.

Battle Honours:

LINCELLES	20 Jun 1811
CORUNNA	9 Oct 1811
BARROSA	9 Oct 1811
PENINSULA	29 Mar 1815
WATERLOO	8 Dec 1815
ALMA	16 Oct 1855
INKERMAN	16 Oct 1855
SEVASTOPOL	16 Oct 1855
BLENHEIM	14 Mar 1882
RAMILLIES	13 Mar 1882
OUDENARDE	13 Mar 1882
MALPLAQUET	13 Mar 1882
DETTINGEN	11 Sep 1882
EGYPT 1882	GO 32/1883
TEL-EL-KEBIR	GO 32/1883
SUAKIN 1885	GO 10/1886

Establishments, Strengths and Locations:

		Offrs	WOs	Sgts	Dmrs	R&F	Total
1st Bn	**Establishment**	35	3	41	16	744	839
	Strength	35	3	41	16	725	820
	Location	Chelsea Barracks, London (arrived Sep 1889)					
2nd Bn	**Establishment**	31	1	41	16	744	833
	Strength	31	1	41	16	721	810
	Location	Wellington Barracks, London (arrived Sep 1889)					
3rd Bn	**Establishment**	31	1	41	16	744	833
	Strength	32	1	41	16	740	830
	Location	Dublin (arrived Sep 1889)					
Depot		Caterham					

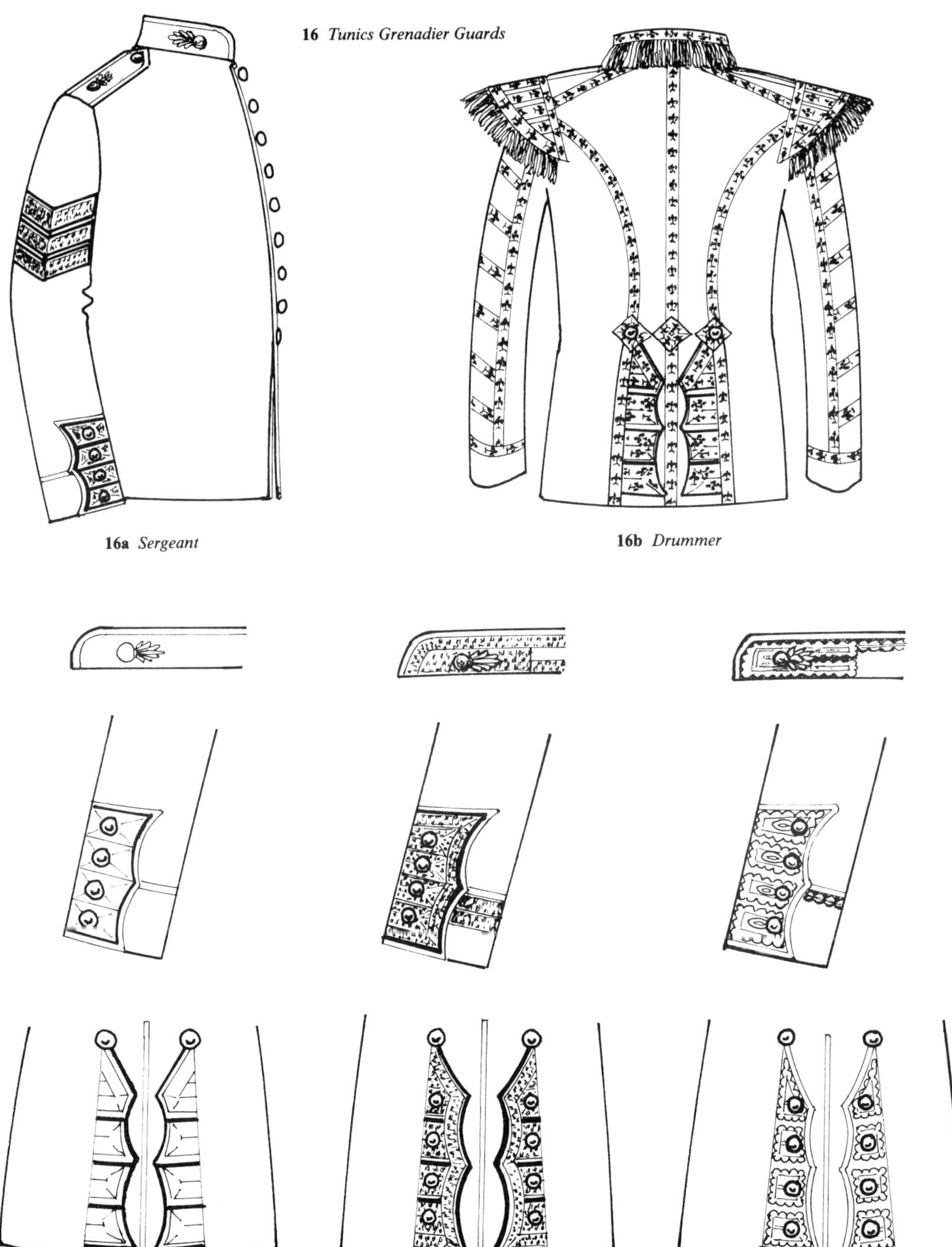

16 *Tunics Grenadier Guards*

16a *Sergeant*

16b *Drummer*

16c *Private*

16d *1st Class*

16e *Lieutenant*

Uniform

The Foot Guards, until 1897, went abroad only on active service. The Grenadiers' 3rd Bn had served, and suffered, in the Crimea and the 1st Bn had spent several years in North America. But more recently two battalions had served in Egypt, the 2nd as part of the Duke of Connaught's Guards Brigade at Tel-el-Kebir in 1882, and the 3rd in the Suakin Expedition of 1885. For both these campaigns, the same medals were awarded which accounts for their presence on all three of Simkin's figures and on several of those in the photographs. The first medal is the Egypt Medal awarded with a variety of bars between 1882 and 1889; it is silver in finish, has a straight bar suspender and its ribbon consists of three blue and two white vertical stripes of equal width. It is almost always accompanied by the Khedive's Star made of bronze with a blackened finish; it has a straight bar suspender with a small crescent attached in the centre, and a plain blue ribbon with no clasps.

The private soldier in Simkin's drawing is in Review Order and seems to be depicted entirely correctly. On the left side of his bearskin was a white horsehair plume. The diagrams in **Fig 16** show the tunic embellishments appropriate to the Grenadier Guards to be added to the description on page 26. It is interesting to note that Simkin's men have the new "Slade-Wallace" equipment and the Lee-Metford rifle; provided this was not his imagination it is likely that his subjects were men of the 1st or 2nd Bns which, being in London, probably received

18 *Colour Sergeant 3rd Bn Grenadier Guards circa 1891*

the new equipment first. The three men awaiting the order to fall in on parade at Wellington Barracks (**Fig 11**) are 1st Bn and confirm Simkin's work; note, however, that they are in Marching Order while his men are in Review Order (with valises). Note also the valise star consisting of the royal cypher within a crowned garter all in yellow metal. By contrast the men of the 3rd Bn shown in **Fig 17**, and photographed about 1891, still have the 1882 pattern valise equipment although they have been issued with the Lee-Metford. That aside, the uniform is the same but note the haversack under the equipment and the Italian pattern water-bottle (visible behind the right elbow) with its strap over everything. Note also the leggings. In the case of both sets of equipment, the waistbelt clasp was of Regimental pattern, made of brass (or gilding metal) with a grenade in the centre.

The Sgt in Simkin's drawing is dressed as shown in the diagram and as described on page 27. His bearskin should have a white horsehair plume. Note that his sash is under his equipment; not visible on his right upper arm are three gold lace chevrons. The CSgt in **Fig 18** wears the same tunic and sash but his waistbelt and pouch are the 1882 pattern. His badge of rank is in full colour (i.e. crown, above a crimson Colour – or flag – embroidered with the Royal Cypher and national emblems in gold, above crossed sabres with gold hilts; pike, pike-head and

17 *Privates 3rd Bn Grenadier Guards circa 1891*

tassels embroidered in gold; all this on a blue ground) super-imposed on three gold lace chevrons – see **Fig 19**. An interesting point which has not so far yielded to research is the reason for the two varieties of Review Order; possibly full equipment was worn for parades and duties outside barracks while a single pouch sufficed for guards and ceremonial within. White gloves seem generally to have been worn by Sergeants and above in Review Order.

19 *Colour Sergeant's badge, Grenadier Guards*

The Captain in Simkin's drawing would have had a white feather plume on the left of his bearskin. His dress is as described on page 30 and the embellishments are illustrated in **Fig 16**. Note that he is wearing white gloves, and the crimson sash and white sword belt appropriate on other than State occasions. His badge of rank was two stars embroidered in silver on each shoulder strap.

The private in drill order in **Fig 17** wears a blue pill-box cap with a scarlet band around the lower part; the badge (a brass grenade) was so positioned that the bottom of the grenade just touched the scarlet; the cap was secured with a patent leather chinstrap. The jacket was quite plain and has been described on page 29. The belt and pouch are the 1882 pattern. He would have been wearing a bayonet frog on his left hip, probably that illustrated in **Fig 8d**.

Finally, the photograph of the drummer boy in **Fig 20** though a well-known picture is still very useful as an illustration of the drum and the drummer's sword, as well as the uniform. Details to note include the shape of the bearskin and plume, though both are wind-blown; the arrangement of drummer's lace and the grenade badge on the shoulder strap; the sword (see **Fig 5a**) in its strapless frog; the blue and white

20 *Drummer, Grenadier Guards circa 1896*

ticken drum-case tied to the cord tensioner on the drum; the drum itself and the arrangement of cord, the Regimental pattern of colours on the hoops, a broad blue line with a white worm (or wavy line) running through it, and a narrow red line above and below; the front of the drum was painted blue and emblazoned (or painted in full heraldic colouring) with the Royal Coat of Arms with flags and banners semi-furled on either side, a gold label above with "? BATT GRENADIER GUARDS" painted on it in black, the Regimental badge below, and the battle honours in black on gold labels in columns on either side. The service chevron on the tunic is correctly "upside-down" so that it remained visible against all the other lace on the sleeve; it is of white worsted on a blue ground. A final curious feature for which no explanation can be offered is the absence of the apron on the left leg which seems to have been out of fashion at that time.

The Coldstream Guards

Titles:

1650–1660	Colonel Monck's Regiment of Foot
1660–1661	The Lord General's Regiment of Foot
1661–1670	The Lord General's Regiment of Foot Guards
1670–1817	Coldstream Regiment of Foot Guards
1817–	Coldstream Guards

Badges:

The Star of the Order of the Garter. Granted in 1695.
The Sphinx superscribed "Egypt". Authorised 6 Jul 1802.

Battle Honours:

EGYPT AND THE SPHINX	6 Jul 1802
LINCELLES	20 Jun 1811
TALAVERA	12 Feb 1812
BARROSA	12 Feb 1812
PENINSULA	8 Apr 1815
WATERLOO	8 Dec 1815
ALMA	16 Oct 1855
INKERMAN	16 Oct 1855
SEVASTOPOL	16 Oct 1855
OUDENARDE	13 Mar 1882
MALPLAQUET	13 Mar 1882
DETTINGEN	11 Sep 1882
EGYPT 1882	GO 32/1883
TEL-EL-KEBIR	GO 32/1883
SUAKIN	GO 10/1886

A Private, Coldstream Guards

Establishments, Strengths and Locations:

		Offrs	WOs	Sgts	Dmrs	R&F	Total
1st Bn	Establishment	35	3	41	16	744	839
	Strength	32	2	41	16	717	808
	Location	Tower of London (arrived Sep 1889)					
2nd Bn	Establishment	31	1	41	16	744	833
	Strength	33	2	40	16	714	805
	Location	Windsor (arrived Sep 1889)					
Depot		Caterham					

Uniform

Like the Grenadiers, the Coldstream had two battalions in Egypt between 1882 and 1885. Clearly, Simkin's subjects were all too young to have served in that campaign, for none wear the medals. It is also interesting to note that both Simkin's private and the subject of **Fig 21** wear the Slade-Wallace equipment. The latter must have been among the first to receive it.

Simkin's private is unremarkable. There would have been a red horsehair plume in the right side of his bearskin. There were nine buttons down the front of his tunic set in pairs with the odd one above the Regimental belt clasp. The embellishments on collar, shoulder straps, cuffs and skirt slashes are illustrated at **Fig 22** and are in line with the general description on page 26. The soldier in **Fig 21** wears the same articles of dress but as he is in marching order, he wears in addition his haversack under the equipment and his water-bottle over it. On the back of his valise would have been a yellow metal plate in the form of a garter star: see *(28)* Figs 43 and 46. He also has a spare magazine pouch on his left brace (see page 22). He wears a single good conduct badge on his left arm, of white worsted on a blue ground.

The drummer is correctly shown by Simkin in his laced tunic. Note in **Figs 23a** and **b**, the shoulder strap with its white rose and the fleur-de-lys lace loops in pairs on the chest and cuffs. Below the fourth pair of loops on the chest, there was one single loop astride the ninth button; in Simkin's drawing the tunic is improperly fitted and this last loop is under the drummer's waistbelt! The drum carriage, as can be seen, was of white buff, and was probably stitched at the end to a brass hook (in Simkin's drawing behind the drummer's left hand);

21 *Private, Coldstream Guards circa 1891*

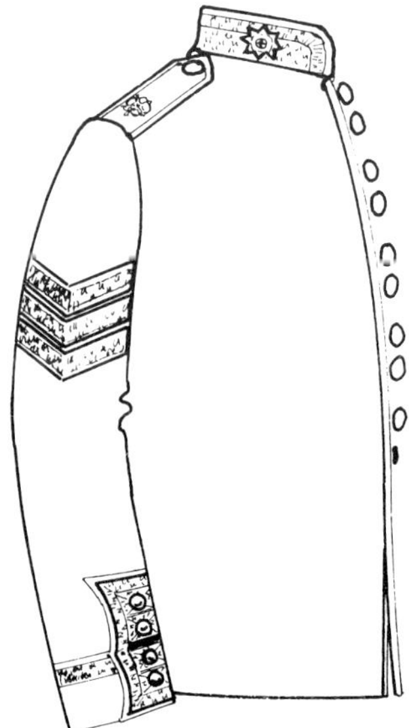

22a *Sergeant Orderly Room Clerk*

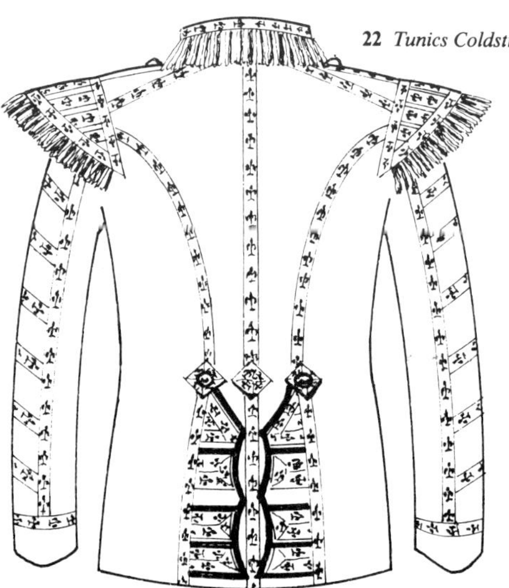

22 *Tunics Coldstream Guards:*

22b *Drummer*

the drum was attached to this hook by a ring and toggle arrangement. Note that the carriage was adjusted by a single prong brass buckle; below it (scarcely visible in the print) was a buff leather runner. The drum is correctly depicted with Coldstream hoops; a blue worm on white, with a narrow red line above and below (though the artist has failed to colour the worm on the lower hoop!). The emblazoning followed the same lines as the Grenadiers' drum described on page 34. Also, it will be observed that Simkin has shown his drummer with an apron of white buff which covered the tunic and trousers from waistbelt to knee, behind which it was secured with three buff leather straps.

Simkin's Lieutenant is as he should be, the match of his Grenadier colleague described on page 34. The particular embellishments of a Coldstream officer's uniform are illustrated in **Figs 22** and **25**, including the single embroidered star of his rank on the shoulder straps. His gilt belt clasp is embellished with a silver garter star. His sword is described on page 00 and illustrated in **Fig 5b**.

Finally, the Sergeant-Major of a Coldstream battalion is photographed in marching order (with undress cap) at **Fig 13**. His forage cap is blue with a gold lace band around the body and gold embroidery on the peak. The cap badge is silver with gilt centre, and there is no chin strap. The tunic is the 1st class type described on page 28 with the Coldstream embellishments illustrated at **Fig 22**. On the collar patches of gold lace, the garter star is embroidered in silver; on the shoulder straps between gold lace edging, the rose is embroidered in silver. The badge of rank cannot be seen but must therefore have been a crown embroidered in full colours on (probably) a scarlet ground, on the right forearm (see also page 28). The sword belt is of white buff, described on page 28 and had a Regimental pattern clasp; the sword is the obsolescent type of Staff Sergeants' weapon with a gilt guard and a black leather scabbard with gilt mounts (see **Fig 4a** and the notes on page 18). The medals are the British award for Egypt 1882, with a single clasp, and the Khedive's bronze star, both described on page 33.

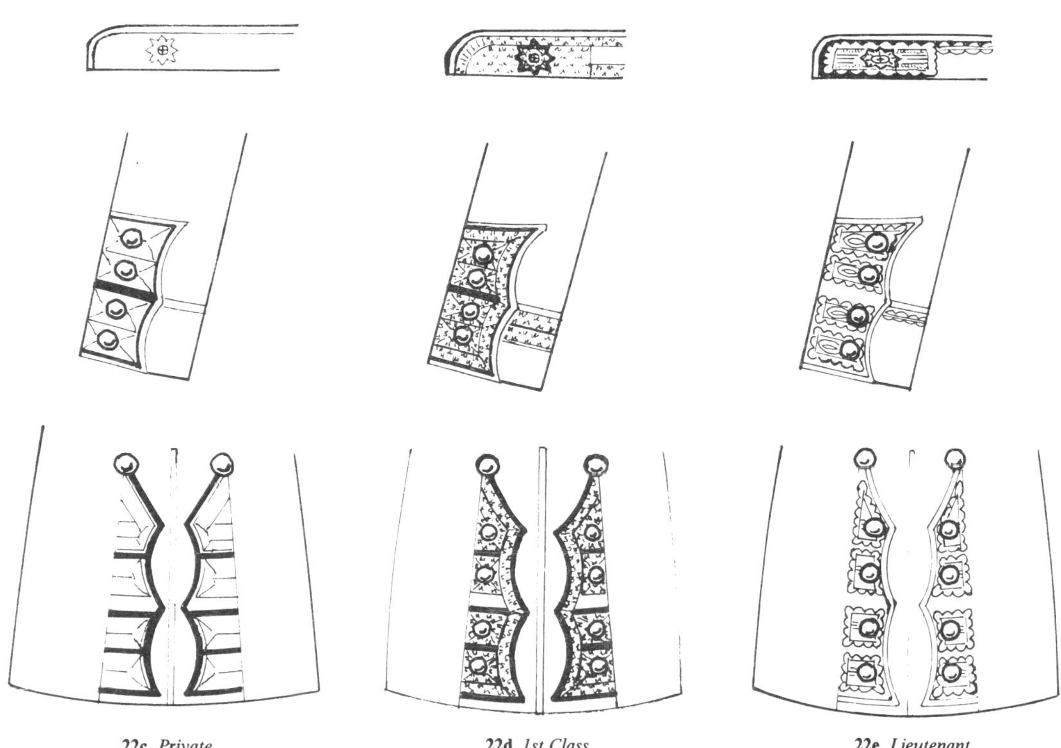

22c *Private*   22d *1st Class*   22e *Lieutenant*

23a *Flautist Coldstream Guards circa 1895 (Army Museums Ogilby Trust)(This photo was tinted which causes the scarlet hackle and tunic to show darker than usual.)*

24 *Colour Sergeant's Badge, Coldstream Guards*

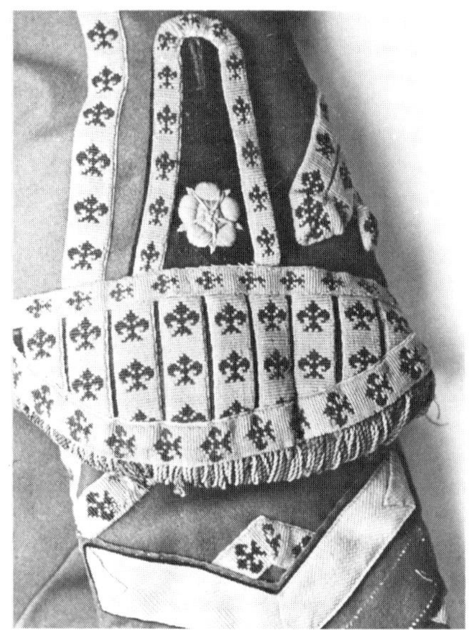

23b *Drummer's tunic circa 1900 (Guards Depot Museum)*

25 *Lieutenant Coldstream Guards circa 1900 (Guards Depot Museum)*

The Scots Guards

Titles:

1641–1650	The Scottish Regiment of Foot Guards
1650–1660	The (King of Scotland's) Life Guard of Foot
1660–1712	The Regiment of Scottish Foot Guards
1712–1831	The Third Regiment of Foot Guards
1831–1877	Scots Fusilier Guards
1877–	Scots Guards

Badges:

The Star of the Order of the Thistle.
The Thistle.
The Sphinx superscribed "Egypt". Authorised 6 Jul 1802.

Battle Honours:

Pioneer, Scots Guards.

EGYPT AND THE SPHINX	6 Jul 1802
LINCELLES	20 Jun 1811
TALAVERA	11 Feb 1812
BARROSA	11 Feb 1812
PENINSULA	6 Apr 1815
WATERLOO	8 Dec 1815
ALMA	16 Oct 1855
INKERMAN	16 Oct 1855
SEVASTOPOL	16 Oct 1855
DETTINGEN	11 Sep 1882
EGYPT 1882	GO 32/1883
TEL-EL-KEBIR	GO 32/1883
SUAKIN 1885	GO 10/1886

Establishments, Strengths and Locations

		Offrs	WOs	Sgts	Dmrs	R&F	Total
1st Bn	Establishment	35	3	42	21	744	845
	Strength	34	3	43	21	752	853
	Location	Wellington Barracks (arrived Jul 1889)					
2nd Bn	Establishment	31	1	42	21	744	839
	Strength	31	1	41	21	707	801
	Location	Chelsea Barracks (arrived Sep 1889)					
Depot		Caterham					

Uniform

It is the tradition in the British Army that seniority is measured from the right. The next senior is at the far end on the left, and the junior in the centre. Had representative battalions of the three Regiments of Foot Guards paraded in line in 1890, it would have been correct for the Grenadiers to be on the right, the Coldstream (not the Coldstreams, incidentally) on the left and the Scots in the centre; this indeed was how they formed up the Guards Brigade at the Battle of Tel-el-Kebir in Sep 1882. The tradition continues on into the battalion itself of which the senior company parades on the right, the next on the left and the remainder in the centre. In all battalions the senior company used to be the Grenadier and the next senior the Light; other companies were referred to as centre or battalion companies. But long before 1890 this terminology had disappeared together with its tactical significance. In nearly all battalions, companies were simply lettered from A to H, though in some they were numbered. However, in the Scots Guards, the Fusilier tradition with its own special form was continued on from 1877 to this day: the senior company is called Right Flank and the next is called Left Flank. So far as

uniform is concerned two details are fairly obvious and are not unconnected with seniority: these are the absence of a plume on the bearskin and the setting of the buttons in threes. Two other features are also distinctive: one is the Scottish connection, as we shall see; the other is the habit on rank and file tunics of plugging a small Regimental button through the centre of the stars on the collar and shoulder strap. The collar was changed from a star to a thistle in 1895 but the habit of wearing a button in the shoulder strap badge continues to this day (the Irish Guards have a similar custom).

With both battalions of the Scots Guards stationed in London, it seems likely that they were among the first to receive the Lee-Metford rifle and the Slade-Wallace valise equipment. Simkin's man has them and his drawing is dated 1890. We know that the 1st and 2nd Bn of the Grenadiers, sharing barracks with the 2nd and 1st Bns, respectively, of the Scots Guards, received theirs in the spring of 1890. It seems reasonable to suppose that both Regiments were issued at the same time. There is nothing remarkable about Simkin's private whose tunic is complimented by that of the Lance Sergeant in

26 *Colour Sergeant Scots Guards circa 1892 (Army Museums Ogilby Trust)*

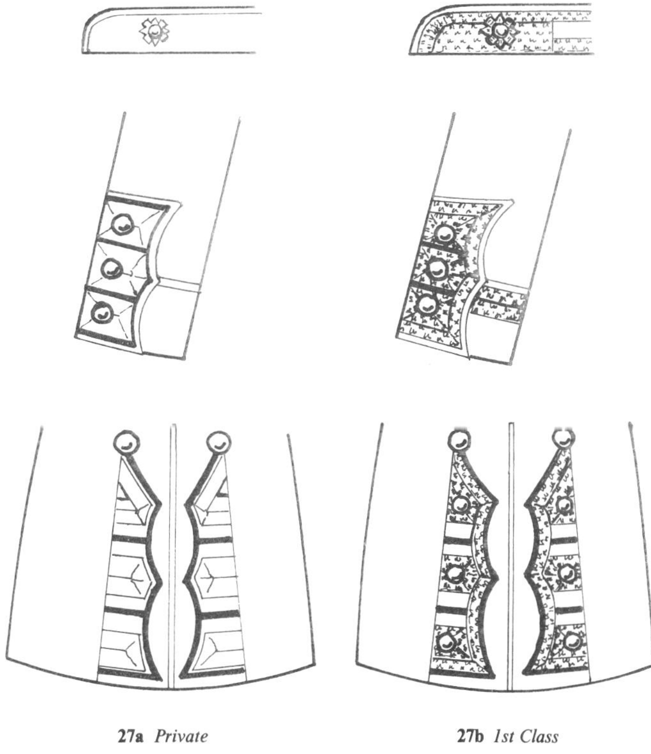

27a *Private*　　　27b *1st Class*

27 *Tunics Scots Guards*

Fig 12. He, incidentally, was a marksman as shown by the worsted (i.e., in this case, white) embroidered crossed rifles on his left forearm. By contrast, the CSgt in **Fig 26** was not only a marksman but also apparently the CSgt of the best shooting company. The latter distinction is shown by the gold embroidered crown over crossed rifles on his right forearm; as a Sgt, his marksman's badge on the left arm is also in gold. Other distinctions of rank (see page 27) include his gold lace chevrons, gold lace loops on his cuffs (and on the skirts behind), silver embroidered Regimental badges on the collar and shoulder straps and of course the crimson sash. Last but not least, his Colour badge illustrated at **Fig 32** consisted of a crown in gold and colours above a crimson Colour (flag) embroidered with a silver star of the Order of the Thistle (in the middle of which the circlet and thistle were embroidered in gold) above a silver Sphinx within a gold wreath; the pike, pike-head and tassels were in gold; the scimitars at the bottom had gold hilts and silver blades.

Simkin's officer is also as he should be with perhaps only two points worth noting. The officer's collar badge was a silver thistle. This contrasted with the white or silver star of the Order of the Thistle worn (as we have noted, until 1895) on the collars of rank and file and Sergeants' class tunics of the men. Wearers of 1st class tunics had, like the officers, a silver embroidered thistle. The other point of interest is that Simkin has given his officer the ordinary crimson silk sash (see **Fig 29**) rather than the gold and crimson variety reserved with different belts and other items for State and Court occasions.

Pipers of the Scots Guards were the only members of the Regiment to wear Highland dress in uniform. A general description is on pages 86–88 but special features are noted below. The headdress was not yet the feather bonnet but still a dark blue glengarry ornamented with a black silk "rosette" on the left or near-side with, on it, a special piper's badge consisting of the star of the Order of the Thistle within a circular strap, all in white metal. Behind the badge was fixed a plume of blackcock feathers. Simkin does not show this and may well have been working from a less than up-to-date photograph; the plume had only been approved for provision at public expense in the spring of the previous year, 1889. The cap was bound with black silk tape which continued at the rear in the form of two tails or ribbons. These were to be of such a length that they would just fail to reach the wearer's eyes when blowing in the wind. The doublet (see **Figs 30** and **31**) was dark blue trimmed

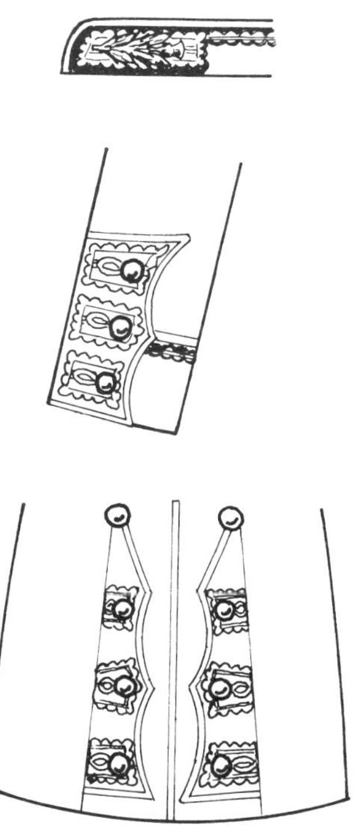

27c Lieutenant

28 *Sergeant Instructor of Musketry Scots Guards circa 1892 (Army Museums Ogilby Trust)*

29 *Second Lieutenant (Ensign) Scots Guards circa 1892 (Army Museums Ogilby Trust)*

30 *Lance Sergeant Piper Scots Guards circa 1892*

with white piping down the chest, on the cuffs, wings and Inverness skirts and on the collar; the latter was most unusual in having besides piping on the top and front, a narrow line of braid from the opening on each side running back in the middle of the collar almost to the shoulder strap, where it ended under a small white metal Regimental button. The kilt and plaid, and the ribbons on the pipes, were Royal Stewart tartan. The hose were green and scarlet diced, secured with scarlet garters; white gaiters secured with white buttons were worn over black shoes in Review Order and in the field, but were discarded in favour of buckled shoes when not on parade with other soldiers. The waistbelt, baldrick and sporran were all of black patent leather with white metal fittings; the waistbelt clasp featured the star of the Order of the Thistle, as did the plaid brooch, and both were in white metal; a silver mounted dirk was worn on the right hip and skean dhu pushed into the right hose. By 1890, the baldrick was an item of traditional dress without practical function. Photographs of pipers wearing claymores are rare but there is some evidence to suggest that the Sgt Piper at least might have done so when on parade with troops under arms. In this event, the claymore,

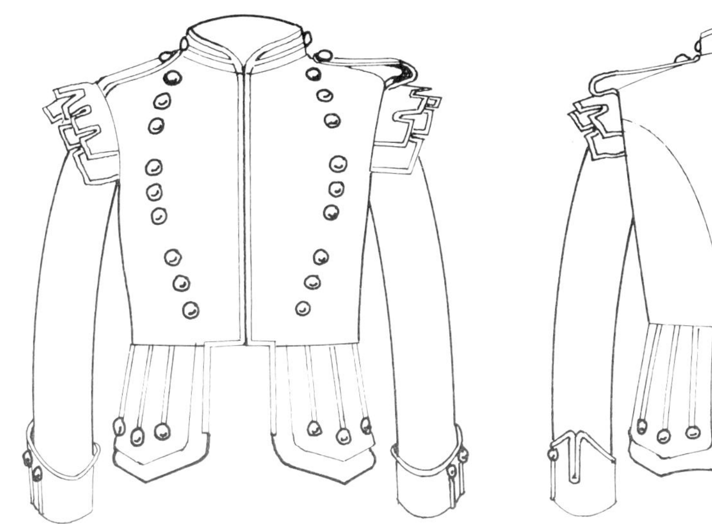

31 *Doublet Piper Scots Guards*

32a *Colour Sergeant's badge Scots Guards*

32b *Valise star Scots Guards*

which had a black leather scabbard with white metal hilt and fittings, was suspended by slings from the waistbelt. The pipes consisted of ebony chanters with ivory fittings, a blue bag with a white fringe at the rear and around the base of each drone, and when appropriate to the occasion a pipe banner. There were many of these and research has so far not yielded a comprehensive list of designs, colours, donors, nor other information. However, it is known that, for example, G Coy 2nd Bn had a plain blue banner at about this time (which is displayed in the Guards Depot Museum at Pirbright) this has a crown in gold and colours above the badge (a gold sala-mander) of the 10th Company above a silver Sphinx within a gold wreath tied with a silver ribbon. (Company badges have been awarded over the years to the Regiments of Foot Guards by the Monarch. They are borne on the Regimental colours of the battalions in rotation as new colours are required and made. So far as the Scots Guards are concerned a compre-hensive list of their use is to be found in the Regimental history "The Scots Guards" by Maj Gen F Maurice published in 1934.) Finally, it is interesting to note that the artist has shown the piper very unusually as left-handed. That is to say, the drones are resting on the right shoulder and the bag is under the right arm, which is the opposite of the normal habit – see Plates 15, 16 and 17. Further, the piper has his right hand above his left on the chanter; had they been the other way around, he would have been said to be "correy-fisted".

THE ENGLISH, WELSH AND IRISH LINE

General Introduction

All armies have their élite formations or units, and the British are no exception. For the Infantry, the top of the social pyramid was occupied by the King's Royal Rifle Corps, or the 60th as they continued to call themselves for nearly a century after the numbers were discontinued. High up the pyramid, by virtue of their closeness to the Sovereign, were the Foot Guards; they were also (and to some extent remain) expensive – which helped. On the upper slopes as well were many of the Scottish Regiments and some of the County Line. But most of the English, Welsh and Irish County Regiments fell into that common category from which the élite regarded themselves as different. But if this induced "chips on the shoulder" they were not often in evidence. Every Regiment, whatever its position in the Army's social pecking order, was a fortress of pride in its own special identity, its own household gods and thus, and most vital, its own Regimental spirit. The Editorial of the first issue of the Green Howards' Regimental magazine entitled "Ours" and published in April 1893 expressed the mood of the day very well;

> "We have, however, . . . a higher motive – old fashioned and out-of-date it may appear to some; an unmeaning, empty phrase to many; to others a sentiment to be ignored, stifled, organised out of existence; to us, an active, living reality – and we call it 'Esprit de Corps'. To foster and promote this feeling in our Regiment is the chief aim of this magazine.

> We take for title our principal theme – and that is 'Ours'. 'Ours' in its glorious past of over two centuries; in its present-day life at home and abroad; in quarters and in the field; in sport and in earnest; 'Ours' by whatever name it has been, is, or shall be known, still 'Ours' – the grand old Regiment to which we are so proud to belong. Our sub-title further explains that 'Ours' is the Gazette of 'The Green Howards' – The name by which the Regiment was distinguished before XIX was embroidered on its colours;

the name whicn survives not only the removal of that number, but even the green facings which gave rise to the title in the days of the gallant Howard.

> Conspicuous on our cover is the Badge of the Royal Lady whose own Regiment we have the honour to be; while, within, resting amid the white roses of our country, lies the old Number, unforgotten."

The numbers, which were supposed by Cardwell to have been put away in 1881, bequeathed seniority and indicated antiquity. The old facing colours if not unique to each battalion were yet special, personal and, since Cardwell, mourned by many. Much effort went into battles to get them back – the Green Howards took eighteen years to win theirs, receiving authority to change from common white back to their ancient green in July 1899. Others took longer: the South Wales Borderers, who as the 24th had also been green but now were white, struggled until March 1905 before success came. The North Staffords had to wait until well after the First World War before recovering the black of the 64th. Perhaps fortunately the Irish Regiments which had been sentenced to green facings by the orders of 1881 were scarcely affected: of the eight, one became Rifles, six more were entitled to the Royal blue, and of the last only one battalion had to change colour for the other was green already (though admittedly a slightly different hue!). It is probably only in Britain that such seemingly unimportant minutiae are regarded as vital – even in the 1980s.

This section looks, therefore, at the great bulk of the "foundation of the British Army" – the English, Welsh and Irish Regiments of the Line. A glance at the full list – *(23)* or *(20)* Army List 1890 – will show a variety of title indicating not merely a territorial affiliation but also qualifications such as "Fusiliers" or "Light Infantry". It should be explained, however, that by 1890 there were no longer organisational or tactical differences between them but merely, as we shall see, those of dress and custom demanded by tradition.

Full Dress Headdress

The common headdress was the home service helmet which was blue for everyone in the Regular Army except Light Infantry who wore green. The only exception to this in dress uniform was the skin cap worn by Fusilier Regiments.

The Home Service Helmet: The helmet was introduced in 1878 and examples (or a variety of modern attempts to copy it) are still in use today with full dress. It was made of cork and covered with cloth including a band ¾ inch wide stitched around the body of the helmet. The soldier's pattern had rounded front and rear peaks bound with leather. The officer's pattern had a pointed front peak bound with gilt metal, a shovel-shaped rear peak bound with leather and a gilt metal bar down the centre of the back from the top to the edge of the peak. The curb chain of brass or gilt ⅝-inch links backed with leather for soldiers or velvet for officers, was attached to brass or gilt rosettes on either side of the helmet. On top was a brass or gilt crosspiece into which a spike was screwed, and on the back was a hook to which the curb chain would be attached when not worn under the chin. The spike and its base stood 3¼ inches high; in the Field Artillery (see page 80 of Volume I) and some of the Departmental Corps (to be described in Volume III) the spike was replaced by a ball in a leaf cup fitting which was 1¾ inches high. The plate on the front was essentially an eight-pointed star, the upper point having been replaced by a crown. A separate circular fitting included the Regimental badge and one of the most obvious differences in Regular Army helmet plates was that the circular fitting was in the centre for officers but noticeably further up towards the crown for soldiers. The helmet plate centre was intended to be (and usually was) backed with scarlet in Royal Regiments.

The Fusilier Cap: The fur cap worn by Fusilier Regiments was of black racoon skin for the men and black bearskin for the officers. The soldiers' cap was about 9 inches tall; the officers' bearskin was of similar proportions to those of the Foot Guards, and was also worn by the WOs and Sgt Dmr of Fusilier battalions. All these caps had a brass or gilt curb chain attached inside the cap, and a grenade Regimental badge on the front. In 1890 only the Northumberland Fusiliers wore a hackle.

Other Ranks' Full Dress

The R&F dress tunic (see the two sentries in **Fig 33**) at this period was scarlet, edged down the front with white piping and fastened with seven brass buttons; there were two further buttons at the waist behind from which two vertical lines of white piping fell to the skirt. The facing colours had been regularised in 1881, as we have noted elsewhere, to blue for Royal Regiments, white for English and Welsh Regiments and green for Irish; these colours were displayed on the low, rounded, collar on which were fixed (in most Regiments) metal Regimental badges – according to the regulations $1\frac{1}{4}$ inches from the opening: the facing colour was also displayed on the plain or "jam-pot" cuffs. The shoulder straps were scarlet and fastened with a small brass button; the Regimental title was embroidered on these in white in abbreviated form for which the factory instructions were: "Titles consisting of initial letters only are to be worked in a straight line and the height is to be $\frac{1}{2}$ inch. Titles consisting of words are to be worked in a half-circle more or less reduced in size according to the number of letters, the size of the letters to be $\frac{5}{16}$ inch." Badges of rank were worn on the right upper arm and good conduct badges (Corporal and below) on the left forearm; all were of white worsted tape on a scarlet ground for all ranks below full Sergeant. Badges of trade or qualification (for example the crossed rifles on the left forearm for a marksman) were embroidered in white or colours on scarlet *(24)*. Trousers were dark blue with $\frac{1}{4}$-inch scarlet welt; they were worn with black boots (which had no toe-cap) and in certain orders with the black leggings.

As in the Foot Guards, there were three basic qualities of tunic; the rank and file pattern described above, the Sergeants' quality and the 1st Class or Staff Sergeants' quality. There were also variations on these patterns for drummers, bandsmen, Sergeant Drummer (or Bugler) and Bandmaster/Band Sergeant. Those concerned with bandsmen are not covered further. The difference for the remainder were as follows:

Sergeants' Class Tunic

This tunic was made of slightly better quality material but to the same design as the rank and file class. The only obvious differences were that badges of rank and proficiency were now made of gold lace or embroidery though still on scarlet backing. Badges of rank were worn on the right arm, with the chevrons above the elbow point downwards. The tunic was worn by:

Rank	Appointment	Badges and Embellishments
Sergeant	—	Three gold lace chevrons on scarlet.
Sergeant	Assistant Instructor of Signalling	Three gold lace chevrons with, above them, crossed signalling flags embroidered in gold and colours, on scarlet.
Sergeant	Instructor of Gymnastics	Three gold lace chevrons with, above them, crossed swords embroidered in gold and silver, on scarlet.
Sergeant	Pioneer	Three gold lace chevrons with above them, crossed axes embroidered in gold and an additional badge worn only by Light Infantry and Fusilier Regts, on scarlet.
Colour Sergeant	—	Three gold lace chevrons with, above them a small crown over crossed Union Flags, all embroidered in gold, silver and colours, on scarlet.

33 Sentries 1st Bn Welsh Regiment circa 1896 (Sergeant in frock; Privates in tunics)

Staff Sergeants' Class Tunic

This tunic was made of better quality material though also to essentially the same design. In addition, however, the collar was edged on the top and front with ½-inch gold lace and along the bottom with gold russia braid; the shoulder straps were edged on the sides and around the top with gold russia braid and the Regimental title was embroidered on each in gold; the cuffs had some form of gold braid embellishment which, according to the regulations and in most Regiments was an edging of ½-inch braid. Badges of rank were worn on the right arm, three bar chevrons point downwards above the elbow and four bar chevrons point upwards on the forearm; the Sergeant-Major's crown was also worn on the right forearm – see **Fig 1**. The tunic was worn by a number of WOs and SSgts of whom the more commonly seen were:

Rank	Appointment	Badges and Embellishments
Quarter Master Sergeant	Regimental Quarter-master Sergeant	Four gold lace chevrons surmounted by an eight-point star embroidered in gold all on a scarlet ground.
Warrant Officer	Sergeant Major	A crown embroidered in gold, silver and colours on a scarlet ground.

Other Dress Distinctions

Sergeants and above wore a (dark) red sash over the right shoulder, meeting just below the waistbelt behind the left hip and ending in tassels which fell to the bottom of the tunic skirts. WOs and SSgts (see page 22) who were not required to wear the standard valise equipment wore instead a white enamelled buff sword belt 1¾ inches wide and fitted with a round yellow metal locket bearing the Royal Crest and Motto. The Sword Staff Sergeants is described on page 18 and illustrated at **Fig 4**.

Drummers

Drummers wore the same full dress headdress as other ranks but the tunic was embellished with drummers' lace which was white worsted ¾ inch wide woven with scarlet imperial crowns at 1⅛-inch intervals (known as "crown and inch" – see **Fig 34**). The collar had this lace along the top and front but, unlike the Foot Guards, also had Regimental collar badges. Crown lace was also laid on the front and rear seams of each sleeve, and on all the seams of the back of the tunic. The wings were scarlet; they were edged with crown lace and crossed diagonally with usually five bars of crown lace. Around the edge of each wing was a fringe of scarlet and white (see **Fig 1**), which was sometimes threaded together and pulled tight making it look rather like striped padding (see **Fig 50**). Officially, there should have been no lace on the cuffs nor (except for Regiments with blue facings) at the base of the collar, but needless to say there were exceptions as can be seen further on. There may also have been instances in which drummers wore the drum badge on the tunic right sleeve, though this was contrary to regulations; the badge was ordered to be worn only on undress jackets. Some Regiments may have provided their drummers with dress cords – in effect, bugle cords which are plaited and looped about the chest in a distinctive way – but they would have been illegal at that time. The earliest case of which the author is

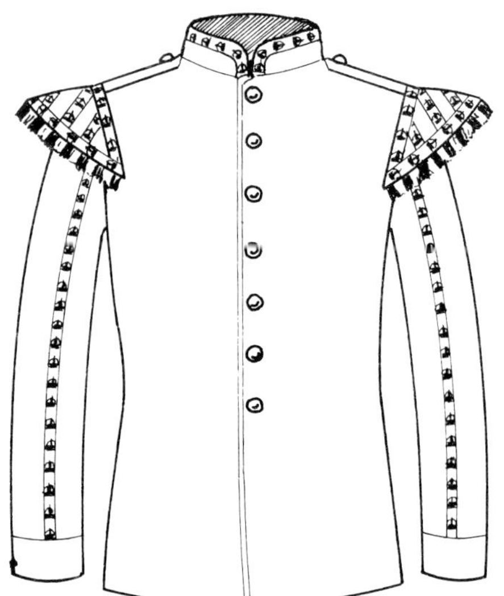
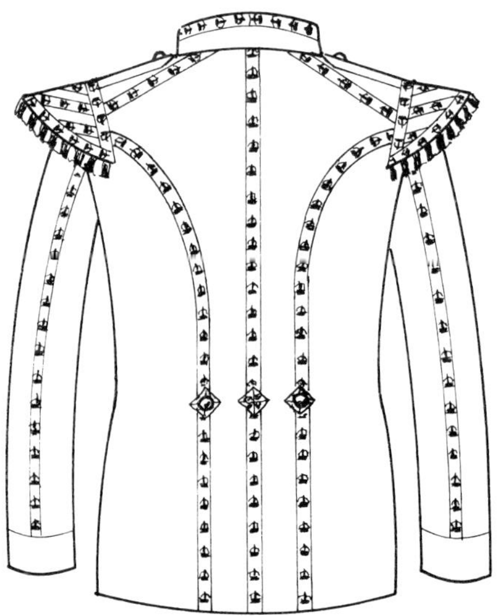

34 *Line Infantry Drummer's tunic*

aware concerned the Dorsets whose 1st Bn drummers were given them in Egypt about 1891; they wore them until moving to India about 1893 when they were summarily ordered to remove them by their new GOC. Finally, in the appropriate orders of dress, drummers wore valise equipment less pouches, but generally with the special drummer's sword.

Sergeant Drummers

There was a distinct tendency among some late nineteenth-century Volunteers to dress their Sgt Dmr up like the proverbial "Christmas tree"; there is sadly something of a similar tendency in the Line today. But in the Line of 1890 this was unknown. As can be seen elsewhere in the book, certain Regiments went in for cuff embellishments on the tunic, and some affected unusual additions to the headdress. Some gave their Sgt Dmr a non-regulation belt and a few possessed unusual staves or maces (of which that carried by the 1st Bn Royal Inniskilling Fusiliers is a good example – see **Fig 54**). These points aside, the Sgt Dmr wore a SSgt's tunic with the customary badge of four gold lace chevrons, point upwards and surmounted by a gold embroidered drum, on a scarlet ground on the right forearm. Like the Foot Guards, he wore gold lace edged and embellished wings but, unlike the Guards, no gold lace on the sleeves nor on the back of the tunic.

Other Ranks' Undress

Headdress: The undress headdress of the day for Sgts (which includes CSgts) and below was a very dark blue glengarry (see **Fig 35**). This was edged with black ribbon which continued from the rear of the cap to form two 11-inch "tails". On top there was a red pompom (a "tuft" or "toorie" as it is called in official documents). A metal Regimental badge was worn on the left of the cap sometimes on a black silk rosette, though the latter was a peculiarity of the by then obsolescent pattern for officers and SSgts. WOs and SSgts wore a dark blue round cap with a near vertical patent leather peak edged with gold embroidery. This had a black purl button on top and around the body (see **Fig 47**) a band of black braid with an oakleaf design or, for (most) Royal Regiments, a band of scarlet cloth instead. On the front was an embroidered Regimental badge provided, according to the regulations, at the soldier's own expense and "similar to" (in other words, the same as!) that worn by the officers.

In contrast to the patterns above, soldiers of Light Infantry Regiments wore a dark green glengarry with a black tuft and black ribbon edging; their SSgts wore a dark green round cap with black button, black oakleaf band and the same, gold embroidered, sharply drooping black patent leather peak as others in the Line.

Jacket: The common undress jacket was called a "frock" of which at this time up to four different types were scaled for issue. These were; the blue recruits' serge jacket, the khaki drill cotton jacket, the scarlet serge frock intended chiefly for service overseas, and the scarlet Kersey tweed or tartan (which were types or grades of woollen cloth) frock for undress wear at home. This latter was a plain scarlet coat cut rather looser than the tunic but of equivalent length, and fastened in the same way with seven brass buttons down the chest. The most obvious difference from the tunic was that the frock had no white piping down the chest nor on the rear skirts. However, that

35 *Sick, Lame and Lazy* – Manoeuvres circa 1890 (Army Museums Ogilby Trust)

aside, several different variations were in issue about this time. The standard one had coloured facings on the collar and cuff (see the Sgt in **Fig 33**) but another, which was trialled from 1889 to 1891 and then abandoned as thoroughly unpopular, had the facing colour on the shoulder straps only (see **Fig 39**). For this pattern the abbreviated Regimental title was embroidered in scarlet on white and green coloured shoulder straps, and in white, as for the tunic, on those of other colours. Some frocks were made and issued with collar, cuffs and shoulder straps in the facing colour (see **Fig 35**) but these were almost certainly discarded not later than 1893. The later patterns of these frocks had pockets with flaps in the front skirts. There was also another pattern made in a slightly shorter style fastening with five buttons down the front; generally they were issued for wear in India and the Colonies, but some no doubt found their way home. Nonetheless, it has to be said that much research remains to be done in this area and a definitive study of Infantry undress clothing would prove a welcome addition to our knowledge.

Regimental collar badges were worn as on the tunic. Badges of rank were also as on the tunic with one exception; CSgts wore a medium-sized crown (instead of a small crown over crossed Union Flags) above their three chevrons (see Plate 13). 1st Class or SSgts' frocks were laced as tunics. Drummers' frocks should not have been laced but sometimes were; they should, however, have had the drum (or horn in the case of Light Infantry) badge on the right sleeve.

Other Garments: Trousers, boots and leggings, when ordered, were as for full dress.

Officers' Full Dress

The scarlet dress tunic (see **Fig 36**) displayed the Regimental facing colour on the collar and cuffs. Both the latter were embellished with ⅝-inch gold lace (rose design for English and Welsh Regiments, shamrock for Irish) and ⅛-inch gold russia braid, according to rank. Fastened with eight gilt Regimental buttons (one more than the soldier's), the tunic was piped white down the front and had two vertical lines of white piping on the rear skirts falling from two Regimental buttons at the waist. The universal pattern of gold shoulder cords secured with a small Regimental button were worn with badges of rank embroidered in silver and colours: 2Lt, none; Lt, one star; Capt, two stars; Maj, a crown; Lt Col, a star with a crown above. Lace was as follows:

Collar. Within an edging of white piping: 2Lt – Capt: gold lace ⅝ inch wide on the top and front of the collar; gold russia braid along the base. Maj – Col: in addition to the above, a line of gold russia braid forming a series of eyes just below the ⅝-inch lace.

Cuffs. 2Lt – Lt: ⅝-inch lace around the top with gold russia braid above and below with ⅜-inch spacing forming a crow's foot and additional eye below and an austrian knot above. Capt: as above except that there were two rows of ⅝-inch lace with ¼-inch "light" of facing colour between the rows. Maj: as for Capt except that the upper line of russia braid was in the form of a row of eyes. Lt Col: as for Capt except that both upper and lower lines of russia braid were in the form of a row of eyes.

In most orders of dress, officers wore trousers or overalls which were blue with ¼-inch scarlet welts. The Commanding Officer, the senior Major (or, possibly, both the Left and Right Majors) and the Adjutant were mounted and wore blue breeches and black knee boots. All officers wore a white buff sword belt which fastened with a round gilt clasp, or locket, of Regimental design and carried slings and a hook for the sword. Mounted officers had additional slings (see Plate 12) for a sabretache. With these articles, officers wore a crimson silk sash over the left shoulder, white gloves and the dress (gold lace with crimson central line, with gold acorn) sword knot. At levies, balls and on State occasions when not on duty with troops, certain other articles were worn (see **Fig 43**); trousers with gold lace stripes 1⅜ inches wide incorporating a central crimson line, a sash 2½ inches wide consisting of three gold and two crimson stripes with gold and crimson runner and tassels, and a gold lace sword belt 1½ inches wide incorporating a common gilt clasp with the Royal Crest (lion over crown) in silver in the centre. The lace on the belt was the same as on the trousers and was laid on red morocco leather. The sword slings were 1 inch wide and the sabretache slings ¾ inch wide.

Officers' Undress

Headdress: Officers of Line Infantry might have been seen at the time with which we are concerned in any of four different undress caps. Most common was the round peaked cap as described on page 47 for WOs and SSgts; it was not provided with a chinstrap and was only very rarely worn with one. The glengarry was still (Dress Regulations 1891) the forage cap laid down for active service and peace manoeuvres; this was as described for WOs and SSgts though the badge in most cases was either different or of precious metal. However, the glengarry seems to have been very rarely used and instead officers wore either the round cap or one of the two types of so-called "austrian" cap. One was known as the "Torin" (see **Fig 37**) and seems to have appeared first in the Crimea War. The other was probably worn for the first time about 1891 and was called then the "field service cap". It was designed and made up as a foldaway balaclava helmet which fastened with two small Regimental buttons. Like the Torin it was made in different colours for different Regiments but eventually became the standard khaki undress cap of the Second World War. Throughout the period it tended to be worn towards the right of the head though it was not entirely for this reason that it was worn by some in the 1890s with a chinstrap. It was and remains (for it is still commonly worn by officers and some soldiers today) a handy, comfortable, colourful but rather perilous item of headgear – even though it is now worn on the centre of the head. Nonetheless habit dies hard for it is known to officers at any rate, as a "side-cap"; soldiers sometimes call it a "chip bag", which it strongly resembles, or something else (which does not bear printing) which it does not!

Jacket: Three jackets were is use at this period. The old dark

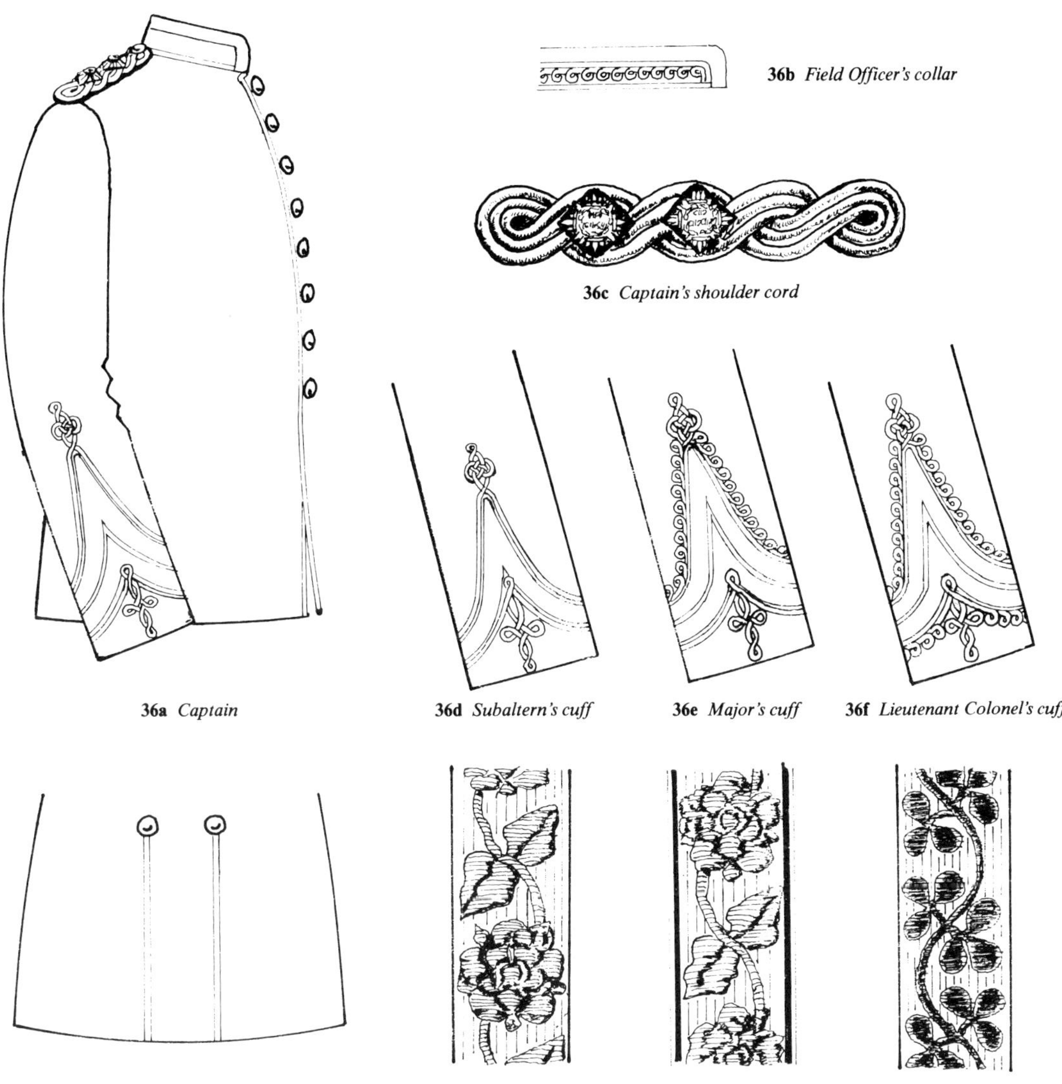

36a *Captain*

36b *Field Officer's collar*

36c *Captain's shoulder cord*

36d *Subaltern's cuff*

36e *Major's cuff*

36f *Lieutenant Colonel's cuff*

36g *English Regiments lace*

36h *English Regiments mourning lace*

36i *Irish Regiments lace*

37 *Captain (Green Howards) circa 1891, wearing Torin Cap (The Green Howards Museum)*

chevron as well. The third was a scarlet patrol jacket which was introduced about 1890. It is shown in Plate 11 and in **Fig 72**, and was cut fairly loose with the collar, shoulder straps and pointed cuffs in the Regimental facing colour. There were two patch pockets on the chest with flaps which seem to have been cut in a variety of ways but were secured with a medium Regimental button; five more such buttons fastened the jacket down the front. There was no lace at all and no Regimental badge was to be worn on the collar; the only embellishment was the badge of rank worn on the shoulder strap and usually of gilt metal. Note that medal ribbons, if worn, began in line with the inner edge of the left pocket and were not, as present regulations have it, centred on the button.

Other Garments: Trousers, boots and accoutrements were as for full dress.

White Helmets

Several of Simkin's drawings in the Army & Navy Gazette series, including some in this book, show men wearing a particular type of white helmet. This headdress which had a distinctive flared brim and was fitted with a yellow metal chin chain, spike and full dress helmet plate, was issued to a number of Regiments at home in or about 1889. It seems to have been a trial which was abandoned probably in 1891, but the object and extent have yet to be fully confirmed by research.

It is thought that it began with attempts to standardise the design of the white or foreign pattern helmet with that of the (blue and green) home service pattern. The original 1878 design of the latter was modified several times to improve it but there was also a clear attempt to incorporate certain desirable

blue patrol jacket with its black mohair braid and frogging (see **Figs 37** and **38** and elsewhere) was about to be abolished. It was probably the most literally uniform jacket ever worn in the British Army, at least until modern times. It had no Regimental badges or buttons and in 1890 was the same for field and junior officers of all infantry Regiments except Rifles. Badges of rank were of gilt metal or gold embroidery and were worn on the shoulder straps. Officers who had been to India may still have possessed the scarlet patrol jacket approved for wear out there (see Plate 4 and **Fig 42**). By comparison with the dress tunic, this was a loose garment. It was scarlet except for the collar which, according to the regulations, was to be in the facing colour. It was rounded in front, had vents behind and had white piping all round except the collar. It was fastened with five Regimental buttons down the front and two more secured scarlet shoulder straps. Badges of rank were embroidered in gold on the shoulder straps which were piped all round in white, and a further indication of rank was given by the arrangement of gold russia braid on the cuffs: Lts had a single chevron of braid (edging, in other words, an imaginary pointed cuff) forming an austrian knot above and a crow's foot and eye below; Capts had two chevrons of braid ¾ inch apart with the same austrian knot and crow's foot and eye; Majs were as for Capts but with a row of eyes formed above the upper chevron, while Colonels had eyes below the lower

38 *Officer's blue patrol jacket (National Army Museum)*

features of the then current foreign pattern. A "khaki" service dress including a helmet for daily wear at home and abroad was trialled in 1884 and while it was soon thrown out principally by the traditionalist lobby, the idea of at least a standard pattern headdress gained a little more ground. It was under active discussion the following year and in Jan 1887 even the Duke of Cambridge, a noted conservative, thought that such a helmet "should become the standard for Home and Foreign service and that possibly white helmets may eventually be worn universally". But nothing was to be done without a trial. It seems that this was the idea behind the distribution in 1889 of some at least of 25,000 white helmets procured from contract during the early summer of that year. Unfortunately no conclusive record has yet been traced of the battalions to which they were issued. In his illustrated booklet of 1890 entitled "Our Armies" Richard Simkin possibly had the broad answer to this question when he said that they were the Line battalions earmarked in peace for the 1st Army Corps, should it be mobilised. However, research in the Clothing Department files shows that the Duke of Cambridge was unhappy with the latest or trial pattern of white helmet even before the 25,000 were received from contract (which led to a desperate last-minute, but abortive, attempt to cancel it!); nor was it much help that the Queen was said to disapprove of the blue version of the same pattern. Thus by the late summer of 1889, it was clear that a white helmet was not after all considered suitable at home, but on the other hand there was now no decision as what pattern of blue and green helmet was to be worn instead. Until this was given, no contracts were let and Line battalions began to run out of helmets. Eventually, in early 1891 it was decided to revert to the 1886 modification of the 1878 pattern; in the meantime, the author concludes, the Clothing Department could do little but issue the white helmets obtained for trial. Although fresh supplies of blue and green helmets were available later in 1891, it seems likely that white helmets were being issued "to exhaustion" (of stock) for at least another year and were to be seen in units as late as 1895 or 1896. Following this conjecture, the author was not surprised to have found that some 1st Army Corps battalions did not have white helmets and similarly that some battalions which had received them (for example 1st Bn The Northamptonshire Regiment in the early summer of 1889) were not earmarked for the Corps.

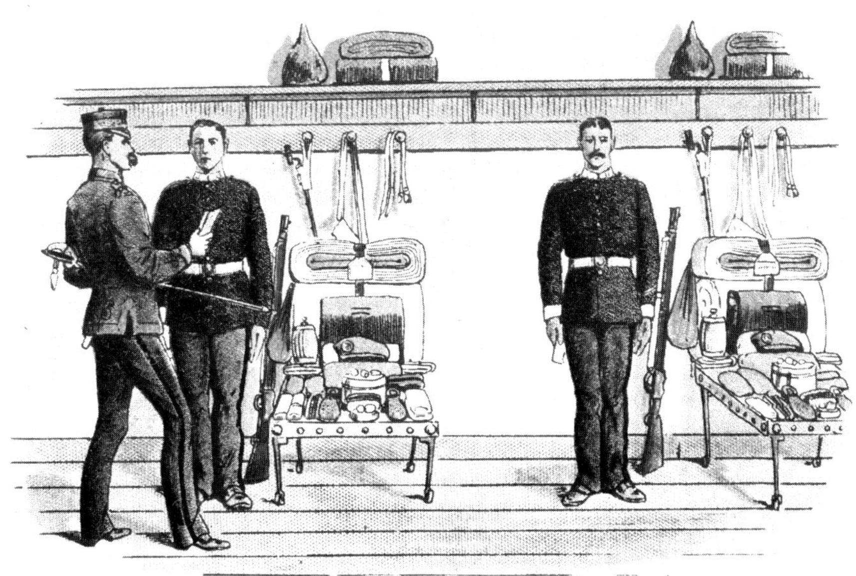

The barrack room. Inspection of kits.

The Buffs (East Kent Regiment)

Titles:

1572–1689	The Holland Regiment (its early years were in Dutch service)
1689–1708	Prince George of Denmark's Regiment
1708–1751	(By the Colonel's name) First official use of the title "The Buffs" was in 1747
1751–1782	The 3rd (or The Buffs) Regiment of Foot
1782–1881	The 3rd (East Kent) Regiment of Foot (The Buffs)
1881–1935	The Buffs (East Kent Regiment)
1935–1965	The Buffs (Royal East Kent Regiment)

Amalgamation with Queen's Own Royal West Kent Regiment

1961–1966	The Queen's Own Buffs, The Royal Kent Regiment

Absorbed into The Queen's Regiment

1966–1969	2nd Bn The Queen's Regiment (Queen's Own Buffs)
1969–	2nd Bn The Queen's Regiment

39 *Privates The Buffs circa 1891 (Army Museums Ogilby Trust)*

Badges:

The Green Dragon.
The Rose and Crown.
Motto. "Veteri Frondescit Honore". (First appeared in the Army List of 1890.)

Battle Honours:

DOURO	10 Sep 1813	SEVASTOPOL	16 Oct 1855
PENINSULA	6 Apr 1815	TAKU FORTS	4 Nov 1861
TALAVERA	4 Jan 1823	BLENHEIM	13 Mar 1882
ALBUHERA	4 Jan 1823	RAMILLIES	13 Mar 1882
PYRENEES	4 Jan 1823	OUDENARDE	13 Mar 1882
NIVELLE	4 Jan 1823	MALPLAQUET	13 Mar 1882
NIVE	4 Jan 1823	SOUTH AFRICA 1879	25 Jul 1882
PUNNIAR	22 Jan 1844	DETTINGEN	11 Sep 1882

Establishments, Strengths and Locations

		Offrs	WOs	Sgts	Dmrs	R&F	Total
1st Bn	**Establishment**	28	2	45	16	920	1011
	Strength	27	2	39	14	982	1074
	Location	Dum Dum, Bengal (arrived Mar 1886)					
2nd Bn	**Establishment**	24	2	39	16	720	801
	Strength	24	2	38	14	602	680
	Location	Aldershot (arrived Aug 1889)					
Depot		Canterbury					

Uniform

By no means the only Regiment with buff facings, the Buffs were nonetheless very proud of theirs and thus their distinctive title. In fact buff was not the pale yellow-brown that the layman might expect but was more pink in tone; it was even referred to at times as "flesh". However, in early 1890 the Regiment was still trying to get its tunics issued with buff facings having lost the colour in 1881 as part of the Cardwell standardisation reforms. For several years, they wore white facings until much lobbying secured permission in April 1887 to colour them buff with a pipeclay mixture. Three years later a change of material was approved but it took a further four

years actually to appear. When it did, in 1894, it was so dark that the pipeclay mixture had to be kept in use but this time to lighten the shade. Simkin did his drawing in 1890 and was therefore correct to show coloured facings but they are probably a little too yellow.

It is doubtful whether either battalion of the Buffs received the Slade-Wallace equipment in 1890 though the 2nd, at home, were probably issued with the Lee-Metford that year. **Fig 39** shows two soldiers of the 2nd Bn about 1891 with the new rifle but the old, 1882, valise equipment. It is interesting to note that they are wearing the ill-fated and unpopular scarlet frock

40 Guard 2nd Bn The Buffs circa 1897

41 *Maxim Detachment 2nd Bn The Buffs circa 1897*

42 *Officers The Buffs, Malta circa 1885 (Army Museums Ogilby Trust)*

which displayed the facing colour only on the shoulder straps.
It is not clear what colour these were but (see page 48) there is
no sign of a dark Regimental title which would have indicated
that they were white. Thus it seems possible that they were buff
with white titles which would not have stood out in a photograph taken from this angle. Other points of interest in **Fig 39**
are the collar badges, with represent the "White Horse and
'Invicta'" and are a pair facing inwards, made of white metal.
(Oddly enough, where a white horse was concerned, these
badges were at first ordered to be made of yellow metal!) For
some years up to 1881, the collar badge had been a dragon, and
this was restored in 1894. In the meantime, this ancient Buffs
badge had survived in the centre of the helmet plate in yellow
metal. The centre of the helmet plate together with a small
crown was worn as the glengarry badge *(10)*.

The frock shown by Simkin is much the same as that worn
by the soldiers of the Buffs in **Figs 40** and **41** (though these
photographs were probably taken about 1897). Note the
facings on collar and cuffs only and the total absence of white
piping. Simkin has missed them from his private but the scarlet
shoulder straps were embroidered in white with "E KENT"
(until about 1889 when they were changed to "BUFFS"). In
both cases the title was slightly curved. All the men are wearing
the dark blue field cap introduced about 1894, with a yellow
metal dragon badge and two small Regimental buttons in
front. The drummer wears a plain frock with the drum badge
embroidered (in yellow with the hoops in blue and the head
and ropes picked out in white) on a scarlet ground on the right
arm; his bugle cord is green. He wears Slade-Wallace valise
equipment but without pouches and, oddly, without a
water-bottle.

Simkin's officer wears his India pattern serge, as was permitted at home until the garment was worn out. The buff collar
was plain apart from the badge of a silver embroidered white
horse over a gold motto "Invicta". The shoulder straps and
badge of rank, together with the gold lace on the scarlet cuffs,
are correct according to the regulations (see page 50). However, at least one battalion of the Regiment had chosen to
affect buff cuffs (see **Fig 42**). The round forage cap worn by
officers (as well as by WOs and Staff Sergeants) was blue and
entirely in line with the regulations (see page 47); the dragon
badge was embroidered in gold.

43 *Lieutenant The Buffs circa 1890 (Army Museums Ogilby Trust)*

The officer in **Fig 43** wears the full dress of about 1890, with
the white helmet which was *de rigueur* in Malta and the
Colonies. The centre of the gilt helmet plate has the dragon in
silver on a black velvet ground. Other items of his uniform are
as described elsewhere but note that he is wearing the sash and
sword belt prescribed for State occasions (see page 48).

The Northumberland Fusiliers

Titles:

1674–1688	Known as a "Holland Regiment", in the service of the Prince of Orange, and by the Colonel's name
1688–1751	By the Colonel's name
1751–1782	The 5th Regiment of Foot
1782–1836	The 5th or Northumberland Regiment of Foot
1836–1881	The 5th or Northumberland Fusiliers Regiment of Foot
1881–1935	The Northumberland Fusiliers
1935–1968	The Royal Northumberland Fusiliers

Absorbed into The Royal Regiment of Fusiliers

1968–	The Royal Regiment of Fusiliers

Badges:

St George and the Dragon.

A red over white plume. Authorised 17 Jun 1829.

The King's Crest and the Red and White Rose. Authorised 27 Mar 1868.

The Rose slipped with the Crown over. Authorised in the Royal Warrant of 1751 concerning Regimental Colours.

The Motto: "Quo Fata Vocant". Authorised 31 Mar 1831.

Battle Honours:

PENINSULA	5 Apr 1815		
ROLEIA	25 Sep 1817	TOULOUSE	28 May 1818
CUIDAD RODRIGO	25 Sep 1817	VIMIERA	10 Dec 1825
VITTORIA	25 Sep 1817	BUSACO	10 Dec 1825
SALAMANCA	25 Sep 1817	CORUNNA	20 Dec 1825
NIVELLE	25 Sep 1817	WILHELMSTAHL	7 May 1836
BADAJOZ	28 May 1818	LUCKNOW	3 Sep 1863
ORTHES	28 May 1818	AFGHANISTAN 1887–80	GO 56/1881

44 *Sergeants 2nd Bn Northumberland Fusiliers 1898*

Establishments, Strengths and Locations

		Offrs	WOs	Sgts	Dmrs	R&F	Total
1st Bn	**Establishment**	24	2	39	16	720	801
	Strength	24	2	39	16	629	710
	Location	Woolwich (arrived Aug 1889)					
2nd Bn	**Establishment**	28	2	45	16	920	1011
	Strength	26	2	47	14	961	1050
	Location	Rawal Pindi, Bengal (arrived Feb 1880)					
Depot		Newcastle-on-Tyne					

Uniform

Aside from their seniority in the Infantry the principal distinction of the Northumberland Fusiliers at this time was their hackle. They were the only Fusiliers to be allowed to wear one and the story of the unusual red over white colours is interesting. At the capture of St Lucia from the French in 1778, the Regiment defeated an enemy reputed to be nine times as strong. In triumph, soldiers of the 5th took white feathers from the headdress of dead French grenadiers – and thus launched a custom which lasted for the next fifty years. It was unusual because the greater part of the rest of the Infantry was wearing red and white plumes, white being the preserve of (British, as well as French) grenadiers alone. In 1829, all the Infantry, except Rifles and Light Infantry, were ordered to adopt the white feather. This put the 5th back with the "herd" and so they applied to maintain their distinction by changing to the red and white plume themselves. It was duly authorised by Horse Guards (i.e. Army Headquarters) letter of 11 Jul 1829.

In his drawing, Simkin shows a pioneer of the Regiment in a very distinctive white apron with the right bottom corner turned forward and secured with a yellow metal grenade on a scarlet backing. Unfortunately, the author has been unable to find any evidence of such a peculiarity at this time. Photographs of the Regiment are particularly rare but a series taken at the St George's Day Parade of the 2nd Bn at Portland in 1898, and published in the Navy and Army Illustrated (for an example see **Fig 44**) although comprehensive show no pioneers in white aprons. From this and the fact that Regimental Headquarters have no information on the subject, the author is driven towards the suspicion that white aprons in the 1890s were either a short-lived 1st Bn eccentricity, or a figment of Simkin's imagination.

The uniforms of Simkin's officer and private are according to the regulations; so too, apart from the apron, is that of the pioneer. In his case, both the beard and the grenade above the crossed axes were correct. Both soldiers, interestingly, have been drawn wearing the 1882 pattern waistbelt. So too, it seems, is the Corporal in **Fig 45** though in his case it is difficult to be certain as the illustration is taken from a tinted photograph which may have obscured rather than illuminated the details. We do not know when either battalion received the 1888 pattern but about 1892 seems likely for the 1st Bn while the 2nd Bn may have had to wait some while longer. It is, however, known that the Lee-Metford was issued to the 1st Bn at Woolwich on St George's Day 1890 and to the 2nd Bn in

45 *Corporal Northumberland Fusiliers circa 1892*

India on 29 Nov 1892. The cap badge is a grenade with the figure of St George and the Dragon within a strap "Quo Fata Vocant" embossed on the bomb *(10)*. The collar badge is a small, plain, brass grenade of the same pattern as that worn by RA (see Volume I) and the scarlet shoulder straps were embroidered in white with a grenade over the "NF". The author can offer no clear explanation for the absence of a plume from the Corporal's cap (in **Fig 45**). The soldier is in Review Order (see page 25) and should have been wearing it; this may therefore have been another casualty to the tinting artist's brush.

Simkin's officer would be wearing a grenade badge in his bearskin much the same as that of his men, but of gilt. His collar badges were gold embroidered grenades with St George and the Dragon in silver on the bomb. His plume is bigger than that of the men, being made of cut feathers rather than horsehair.

To end, several features of **Fig 44** deserve further explanation. All ranks wear a red and a white rose in their headdress while the Sgt Dmr on the left has more roses entwined on his staff; this was a Regimental custom observed on St George's Day, 23 April, every year. The WOs and SSgts wear the round, peaked, forage cap, while the four officers present and the Sgts wear the blue field service cap. It would be instructive to note the ranks and appointments of all those present but this is not possible as many of the badges cannot be seen. However, one can make a reasonable attempt at the first two rows. Seated on the ground, from the left; a SSgt (no badge of appointment and therefore probably an Orderly Room Clerk ranking as Sgt), a Sgt (who appears to have a brassard on his left cuff and was thus the Battalion Provost Sergeant), a Sgt who was evidently the Assistant Instructor of Signalling, and another SSgt. In the second row, seated on chairs, are from the left: the Sergeant Instructor of Musketry (who was a SSgt and wore a crown over crossed rifles in gold above his chevrons of rank as his badge of appointment), the Sergeant Major, four officers (of whom the first two are evidently more senior than the others but whose rank cannot be given for certain because of the poor quality of the picture), the Bandmaster and the Quartermaster Sergeant (whose badge of a gold star above four chevrons point uppermost can just be seen). Finally the Sgt Dmr on the left has some interesting attributes: the hackle on his bearskin is enormous reaching from low on the left side right over the cap, the part across the top being scarlet; the white "blob" on the front of his cap is of course a rose; the staff is obviously a Regimental special but its design and present location seem to be a mystery. The sash or belt is the pre-1881 pattern retained no doubt because of its green colour; in addition to the gold lace edging, the white metal plate bearing the two miniature drumsticks and the gold embroidered "VR" cypher, one can see lower down the gold embroidered grenade over the numeral "5". By contrast, the 1st Bn at this period had a "Foot Guards" type of belt which was green and richly embroidered with badges and battle honours.

A Fusilier.

The Princess of Wales's Own (Yorkshire Regiment)

Titles:

1688–1751	By the Colonel's name
1751–1782	The 19th Regiment of Foot
1782–1875	The 19th (1st York North Riding) Regiment of Foot
1875–1881	The 19th (1st York North Riding) Princess of Wales's Own Regiment of Foot
1881–1902	The Princess of Wales's Own (Yorkshire Regiment)
1902–1920	Alexandra, Princess of Wales's Own (Yorkshire Regiment)
1920–	The Green Howards (Alexandra, Princess of Wales's Own Yorkshire Regiment)

Badges:

The White Rose of York.

The Princess of Wales's Cypher and Coronet. Granted 11 Oct 1875.

The Rose. Granted in 1881. Changed to the united Red and White Rose in 1883.

Battle Honours:

ALMA	16 Oct 1855
INKERMAN	16 Oct 1855
SEVASTOPOL	16 Oct 1855
MALPLAQUET	13 Mar 1882

46 *Colonel A J Paterson, Yorkshire Regiment circa 1890 (Green Howards Museum)*

Establishments, Strengths and Locations:

		Offrs	WOs	Sgts	Dmrs	R&F	Total
1st Bn	Establishment	24	2	39	16	720	801
	Strength	23	2	46	16	691	778
	Location	Portsmouth (arrived Sep 1889)					
2nd Bn	Establishment	28	2	45	16	920	1011
	Strength	28	2	39	16	736	821
	Location	Madras (arrived Jan 1890)					
Depot		Richmond, Yorkshire					

Uniform

The Yorkshire Regiment of 1890 is better known today as the Green Howards, an unofficial title until 1920. They acquired it about the time of Dettingen, when commanded by the Honourable Charles Howard, in order to distinguish them from the Buff Howards (later of course, the Buffs) commanded by another (unrelated) Howard. The green facings of that time lasted until 1881 when they were summarily removed by Cardwell; the white, which replaced them, were very unpopular and were eventually dismissed in Jul 1899 when the restoration of green was authorised by the Queen. The official title of 1890 is interesting in that it commemorates permission to style the Regiment "The Princess of Wales's Own" though the Princess was not appointed Colonel in Chief. However, she did allow her cypher and coronet to be used and these became the basis of cap and collar badges for all ranks after 1881. The cypher consists of the stylised letter "A" (for Alexandra) combined with a cross (the Danish Dannebrog), in the centre of which is the date, 1875, on which its use was authorised to the Regiment. Above the cypher was the Princess's coronet, all well illustrated in **Fig 46**.

Simkin's drawing shows a familiar duo, the Commanding Officer of a battalion and his Regimental Sergeant Major or RSM. (Readers in the United States in particular may be confused by the use of the term "Regimental" in this context. Although it is a battalion appointment and there were, for example, six RSMs in the Yorkshire Regiment of 1890, the term has never changed and continues throughout the Army to this day).

The photograph of Sergeant Major Hughes in **Fig 47** shows the detail upon which Simkin's drawing might have been based – even down to the medals! The Sergeant Major would have worn an other ranks' helmet, but might well have been provided with an officer's badge. Mr Hughes is wearing the

47 *Sergeant Major Hughes, Yorkshire Regiment circa 1897 (Green Howards)*

48 *Types 1st Bn Yorkshire Regiment circa 1891*

dark blue forage cap for WOs and SSgts (which was the same for officers) with the black oakleaf braid, the small black, gold embroidered, peak and the embroidered badge; the cross in silver edged with crimson, and the "A", the coronet and the "1875" in gold, all on a blue ground. The collar badges are also the same as for officers and a simpler version of the cap badge: the cypher and coronet embroidered in gold, and the cross in silver. Note that the shoulder title "YORK" is embroidered in gold and slightly curved.

Simkin's Commanding Officer is in a sense a cheat! Not one of the four regular and militia battalion COs had any active service and therefore none had any medals. **Fig 46** shows, for example, Col A J Paterson who was commanding the 1st Bn in 1890. That (probably unfair) comment aside, Simkin's officer is entirely in accordance with the regulations and no doubt with practice in this Regiment. Note the evidence of rank to be seen in the embroidery on the collar and cuffs (also **Fig 36**) and in the badges on the shoulder cords. The white buff belt would have been fastened with a round gilt clasp incorporating the cypher and coronet also in gilt and the cross in silver; five white buff slings supported the plain black leather sabretache of a field officer and the sword with its brass scabbard. The sword knot on the gilt hilt was gold cord with a gold acorn, and the spurs on the black boots were brass. The horse furniture was simple and has been drawn in accordance with the regulations – see page 24.

Although Simkin shows no junior ranks, **Fig 48** has been included to give a view across the Regiment. It is a well-known photograph published several times since it was taken, possibly towards the end of 1892. But with apologies to those readers and collectors who know it well, the author feels it is worth producing again not least because it has so many interesting points. The men are of the 1st Bn and are wearing the normal seven-button frock with white collar and cuffs. They all wear too the scarlet button-on patch on the left breast developed to protect the white buff straps and, to a lesser extent the jacket, from oil stains when the rifle was carried at the left shoulder. The Lee-Metford had been issued, incidentally, to the 1st Bn at Portsmouth in about March 1892 and to the 2nd Bn in Burma on 7 Apr 1893. More interesting though is the relatively unusual practice of wearing the 1882 valise equipment with 1888 pattern pouches. The 1st Bn did not receive the full Slade-Wallace 1888 pattern equipment until early 1897 when they were at the Curragh, in Ireland. The pouches were obviously obtained early in order to be able to secure the new .303 ammunition in a manageable way; it would have been impossible to extract it easily and quickly from the much more capacious 1882 pattern pouch. Both Sgts are wearing the sash over the haversack strap, a common practice. Finally, it is worth noting the way in which the abbreviated Regimental title is shown on the valise.

The raw recruit, having a little money about him, and not having as yet received his uniform, some kind friends extemporize a rig-out for him, in order that they may show him the sights of the town and, incidentally, drink his health.

[N.B. Plain clothes not allowed out of barracks.]

The Royal Welsh Fusiliers

Titles:

1688–1714	By the Colonel's name
1714–1727	The Prince of Wales's Own Royal Regiment of Welsh Fusiliers
1727–1751	The Royal Welsh Fusiliers
1751–1881	The 23rd (Royal Welch Fusiliers) Regiment of Foot
1881–1920	The Royal Welsh Fusiliers
1920–	The Royal Welch Fusiliers

Badges:

The Rising Sun.

The Coronet, Plume and Motto of the Prince of Wales.

The Red Dragon.

The Sphinx superscribed "Egypt". Authorised 6 Jul 1802.

The White Horse of Hanover and Motto: "Nec Aspera Terrent".

Battle Honours:

MINDEN	1 Jan 1801	TOULOUSE	15 May 1821
EGYPT AND THE SPHINX	6 Jul 1802	CORUNNA	Feb 1825
PENINSULA	6 Apr 1815	ALMA	16 Oct 1855
WATERLOO	23 Nov 1818	INKERMAN	16 Oct 1855
MARTINIQUE	31 Oct 1816	SEVASTOPOL	16 Oct 1855
ALBUHERA	31 Oct 1816	LUCKNOW	3 Sep 1863
BADAJOZ	15 May 1821	ASHANTEE	18 Oct 1876
SALAMANCA	15 May 1821	BLENHEIM	13 Mar 1882
VITTORIA	15 May 1821	RAMILLIES	13 Mar 1882
PYRENEES	15 May 1821	OUDENARDE	13 Mar 1882
NIVELLE	15 May 1821	MALPLAQUET	13 Mar 1882
ORTHES	15 May 1821	DETTINGEN	11 Sep 1882

Establishments, Strengths and Locations:

		Offrs	WOs	Sgts	Dmrs	R&F	Total
1st Bn	Establishment	28	2	45	16	920	1011
	Strength	28	2	48	14	976	1068
	Location	Lucknow, Bengal (arrived Sep 1880)					
2nd Bn	Establishment	24	2	39	16	720	801
	Strength	24	2	38	16	598	678
	Location	Galway (arrived 1887)					
Depot		Wrexham					

Uniform

The senior Line Regiment of Wales, the Royal Welch Fusiliers (or The "Royal Goats", as they were once nicknamed without much originality) are unusually well equipped with Regimental customs and peculiarities of dress. Seen from the front, regular battalions of the Regiment were (and still are) on ceremonial occasions preceded by their Pioneers in their distinctive aprons – see **Fig 49**. Not far behind, and leading the Band and Drums was (and, again, still is) the battalion's Goat with its drummer handler known as the Goat Major. Then, to be observed from the rear, was another unusual feature, the Flash. This can be seen on Simkin's officer and, less clearly, in **Fig 49**; it is a "fan" of five swallow-tailed black silk ribbons 9 inches long fastened to the back of the collar. It was formally approved in Dec 1834 in memory of the hair queues and their ribbons which the Regiment had worn for some years longer, apparently, than the rest of the Army. Confined to officers,

49 *Types 2nd Bn Royal Welsh Fusiliers circa 1892*

WOs and SSgts in 1890, the custom was extended to all ranks in 1900. The first Goat, however, seems to have marched with the Regiment as early as the late eighteenth century. In 1844, the custom was endorsed by the Sovereign when she presented the first Royal Goat. This animal was selected from a herd descended out of a pair given to the Queen by the Shah of Persia. The Royal Herd has provided the Regiment with a succession of Goats ever since.

Simkin's Sgt Dmr is clearly based on the 2nd Bn personality of the day. The headdress is correctly shown as a bearskin with a yellow metal chin chain; what looks like a white button on the front is in all probability meant to indicate silver Prince of Wales's feathers on a yellow metal or gilt (officer's pattern) grenade badge. There was no white plume or hackle at this time. The tunic is of staff sergeant's quality with gold ½-inch lace on the top and front of the collar and on the wings, with gold russia braid around the shoulder straps and around the base of the collar. The shoulder straps carried a grenade over the letters "RWF" embroidered in gold wire. The trousers, gauntlets and, from what can be seen of them, the belt and sword are correct and as described elsewhere. There now remain a number of areas of doubt in which, for lack of photographs or other clear contemporary evidence, the author has had to fall back on circumstantial evidence or even intuition. First, there are the collar badges; Simkin has indicated these as white metal or silver embroidery, as for an officer. Although there is evidence that such badges were worn by SSgts in the early 1880s, there is none that they were still

being worn in the early 1890s, (see **Fig 50** and **51**). By the end of the decade, the Sgt Dmrs of both regular battalions wore small OR's yellow metal (RA pattern) grenades and the RSM of the 1st Bn wore no collar badge at all on his tunic. The author feels that Simkin may have guessed. Next is the badge of rank,

50 *Sergeant Drummer, Goat and Goat Major 2nd Bn Royal Welsh Fusiliers circa 1897*

shown as the three chevrons of a Sgt with a gold embroidered drum above. Although the Sgt Dmrs of the Infantry had been demoted in rank and style from Drum Major in Oct 1881, no change had been made to their uniform which remained that of a SSgt with the badge of a QMS (previously a 1st class Staff Sergeant). Examples of Sgt Dmrs wearing a Sergeant's badge are known but the author has no evidence of this among regular Infantry, particularly the Royal Welsh. Nonetheless this may not be a Simkin guess. Next is the mace or staff which is unusual in being taller, so it seems, than the regulation 62 inches, secondly in being capped with Prince of Wales's feathers rather than a crown, and thirdly in being of white metal rather than gilt or yellow metal. This is too particular to have been a total invention but RHQ Royal Welch Fusiliers are unable to confirm that such a mace existed. If it did, it had been withdrawn by the end of the decade; in **Fig 50** the 2nd Bn mace is regulation and in **Fig 51** the 1st Bn one, while non-regulation, is apparently very plain and not at all like Simkin's. The author's belief is that Simkin made his drawing from a verbal description and misinterpreted the position of the Prince of Wales's feathers. According to the regulations, they were to be (as for the headdress) superimposed on the bomb of a fusilier grenade on one side of the head of the mace; actually, see **Fig 50**, they seem to be on their own and probably replaced the entire grenade in that position and this may be the source of an error by the artist. The last of the areas of doubt is the ceremonial belt. **Fig 50** is a fair photograph of what the embellishments actually were. On a belt faced with blue cloth and edged with gold lace were, from the top: a crown in gilt and colours; the royal cypher "VR" in gold; silver Prince of Wales's feathers; a silver dragon on a scarlet backing within a gold embroidered scarlet scroll; (looking, in Simkin's drawing, like the flames of a grenade but actually) the Rising Sun in silver upon a scarlet backing; a large scarlet device with battle honours embroidered in gold on small scrolls superimposed on a silver laurel wreath and the White Horse in silver in the centre backed with scarlet and standing on a silver ground; the Sphinx in silver surrounded by more gold embroidered battle honours all mounted on a scarlet backing extending from the bottom of the Sphinx to beneath the lowest scroll; a white metal plate with ebony miniature drumsticks; a gold embroidered grenade. From **Fig 51**, it can be seen that the 1st Bn belt was rather different.

Simkin's goat is unremarkable except perhaps for two points. The silver plate is a little too large and the horns were gilded or sanded and polished, to make a bright show.

The officer is according to regulations which provided for a headdress as described above for the Sgt Dmr, a full dress tunic with silver embroidered grenade collar badges, and a buff waistbelt with a gilt plate featuring the Prince of Wales's plumes or feathers in silver in the centre. Other articles were as described elsewhere.

Some features of individuals shown in **Fig 49** and not so far described are worth noting. The R&F full dress tunic had white piping round the base of the collar but none on the cuffs; the scarlet shoulder straps were embroidered in white with a grenade over "RWF"; other features were as described elsewhere. All three R&F are wearing 1882 pattern valise equipment although they had the Lee-Metford rifle (see comments on page 19 concerning this combination). The Pioneer wore, as ordered, a white grenade above his crossed axes badge of

51 *Sergeant Drummer 1st Bn Royal Welsh Fusiliers circa 1898*

appointment; his apron fastened with a strap behind his neck and was held in at the waist by his belt; the front of the apron was folded up and secured with a brass grenade plate on a piece of scarlet backing cloth. Finally the officer in the dark blue patrol jacket wears the round peaked forage cap with a scarlet band and a gold embroidered grenade badge with the dragon in silver on the bomb. He also has an object in (or beneath) his right hand which the author assumes to be a handkerchief, if carried, gloves should have been brown leather.

The author has tried to avoid including in the book photographs which were taken abroad, but **Fig 50** was unavoidable. However, from it, the reader may wish to note the tropical helmet worn with chin chain, spike and puggaree, but without any badge; this is not the experimental pattern worn at home and mentioned on page 50. The Goat Major shows the drummer's tunic to good advantage, including the wings with threaded fringes, the shoulder straps, collar badges and lacing. Note also the 1888 pattern waistbelt, drummer's sword and the "swagger" stick with its nickel-plated head and tip, essential equipment for every late Victorian and Edwardian soldier. Lastly, it is worth noting the fact that the trousers, if rather baggy, were long enough; today most soldiers, particularly in full dress, wear them at least ½ inch too short and all too often flapping round the ankles!

The Royal Inniskilling Fusiliers

Titles:

1st Battalion
1689–1751	By the Colonel's name
1751–1840	The 27th (Enniskillen) Regiment of Foot
1840–1881	The 27th (Inniskilling) Regiment of Foot

2nd Battalion
1854–1858	The Hon East India Company's 3rd (Madras European) Infantry
1858–1861	The 3rd (Madras) European Infantry Regiment
1861–1881	The 108th (Madras Infantry) Regiment

1881–1968	The Royal Inniskilling Fusiliers

Amalgamation with The Royal Ulster Rifles and The Royal Irish Fusiliers
1969–	The Royal Irish Rangers (27th (Inniskilling) 83rd and 87th)

Badges:

The Castle of Inniskilling, with St George's Colours. An old badge of the 27th.

The White Horse of Hanover and "Nec Aspera Terrent". Authorised to the 27th for service during the Rebellion of 1715.

The Sphinx superscribed "Egypt". Authorised to the 27th, 6 Jul 1802.

Battle Honours:

(1)	EGYPT AND THE SPHINX	6 Jul 1802
(1)	MAIDA	24 Feb 1807
(1)	PENINSULA	6 Apr 1815
(1)	WATERLOO	8 Dec 1815
(1)	BADAJOZ	22 Oct 1821
(1)	SALAMANCA	22 Oct 1821
(1)	VITTORIA	22 Oct 1821
(1)	PYRENEES	22 Oct 1821
(1)	NIVELLE	22 Oct 1821
(1)	ORTHES	22 Oct 1821
(1)	TOULOUSE	22 Oct 1821
(1)	ST LUCIA	28 Mar 1836
(2)	CENTRAL INDIA	3 Sep 1863
(1)	SOUTH AFRICA, 1835	25 Jul 1882
(1)	SOUTH AFRICA, 1846–7	25 Jul 1882

52 *Royal Inniskilling Fusiliers circa 1892. Left to right: Sergeant Drummer, Sergeant Major, Colour Sergeant*

Establishments, Strengths and Locations:

		Offrs	WOs	Sgts	Dmrs	R&F	Total
1st Bn	**Establishment**	24	2	39	16	720	801
	Strength	26	2	38	16	620	702
	Location	Portsmouth (arrived Jan 1889)					
2nd Bn	**Establishment**	28	2	45	16	920	1011
	Strength	29	2	47	14	861	953
	Location	Secunderabad, Madras (arrived Jan 1889)					
Depot		Omagh					

Uniform

The town of Enniskillen is in Ireland and it has a castle. Almost three hundred years ago, King William III raised volunteers in his cause and they defended the town with great gallantry against the King's enemies. Their direct descendants were the 27th or Enniskillen Regiment of Foot. In 1840, "Enniskillen" was exchanged for "Inniskilling" and in the same year the Regiment was given the strikingly unusual staff to be seen in **Figs 52** and **54**; this is engraved around the top: "Presented by The Earl of Enniskillen to his old friends and countrymen The 27th or Inniskilling Regt of Foot July 1st 1840." The precise difference between Enniskillen and Inniskilling is not the only facet of the Irish question to elude the author!

Other ranks of the Inniskilling Fusiliers were dressed generally in accordance with the regulations. Simkin's private wears a rather bulky racoon skin cap correctly equipped with brass chin chain and the brass grenade badge, which featured a three-turreted castle with a circlet inscribed "INNISKIL-LING". There was no plume at this period. (A grey hackle to be worn on the left side was authorised in 1903 as a mark of the Regiment's performance in the South African war and to commemorate the grey coats of its seventeenth-century forefathers). The scarlet tunic had blue facings, the collar having in addition (quite correctly) a line of white tubular piping at the base; Simkin has missed this detail. The collar badge was a small plain brass grenade. The shoulder straps were scarlet and were embroidered in white with a grenade above "INN^G F"; the letters should have been on a curve but from the photographs dated about 1891 they seem to be set in a straight line. In 1891, the 1st Bn was still using the Martini-Henry rifle and the 1882 pattern equipment; it had exchanged both by 1899

but in what year is not known for certain. Note that the CSgt in **Fig 52** is equipped with the long sword bayonet.

No photograph of a drummer of the 2nd Bn at this time has presented itself but those of the 1st Bn (e.g. **Fig 53**) show certain features with which Simkin does not agree. The most obvious of these is the austrian knot of scarlet and white worsted lace on the cuffs; this was unofficial. A second difference lies in the length of the apron. Thirdly, Simkin has given his drummer, probably wrongly, a drum badge on the right sleeve. Finally, he failed to give him a bugle with its Royal Regiments' red, blue and yellow cord and tassels.

Sergeant Drummer Cook (on the left of **Fig 52**) displays his bearskin to good advantage by comparison with the CSgt's smaller racoon skin cap. His tunic is laced with ½-inch gold lace on the top and front of the collar, and on the wings; there is gold russia braid around the base of the collar and around the shoulder straps; the grenade and title are embroidered in gold. The Sergeant Major next to him wears his frock embellished in the same way except that it has the old pattern of detachable shoulder straps which had gold russia braid all round. Note, however, that the Sgt Dmr's cuffs are apparently embellished with a gold russia braid austrian knot (just showing above the gauntlet) and that both he and the Sergeant Major carry the old pattern sword. The belt or sash is, however, the new pattern made of blue cloth and embellished according to the regulations; the lowest device is a blue label embroidered in gold with the Regimental title. The mace is that presented by the Earl of Enniskillen in 1840 and consists of a blackthorn fitted with a silver ferrule, green and buff woollen cords and tassels and, at the top, a silver castle (see **Fig 54**). The

53 *Drummers Royal Inniskilling Fusiliers circa 1892 (Army Museums Ogilby Trust)*

54 *Drum Major's blackthorn staff of the 27th (Inniskilling) Foot, photographed 1983 (Royal Irish Rangers Museum)*

55 *Officers Royal Inniskilling Fusiliers circa 1892 (Army Museums Ogilby Trust)*

latter is interesting in that it should have a central tower with a St George's flag flying. In 1891 (see **Fig 52**) it had only the flag but by 1983 this had gone and was replaced by the tower alone (see **Fig 54**). No explanation for this can be offered for certain.

Simkin's officers are correctly drawn (see **Fig 55**). On the bearskin, the badge is a gilt grenade with the castle in silver on the bomb. The tunic collar badges and the forage cap badge worn by both the officer and the Sergeant Major (**Fig 52**), which were embroidered in gold and silver wire, were similar. Finally, the officers' waistbelt clasp was of a special design which succeeded in packing all the Regiment's badges into a very small space indeed. Briefly the round clasp presented a burnished gilt plate to the front on which there was a gilt grenade bearing a scroll "INNISKILLING" over the castle in silver; below that was the White Horse in silver with the motto "NEC ASPERA TERRANT" in gilt underneath; around these devices was a laurel wreath bearing six battle honour scrolls in silver on each side and, at the bottom, the Sphinx and "EGYPT" in gilt. Finally, the officer in blue patrols is correctly shown by Simkin wearing brown (dog skin) gloves.

The Duke of Wellington's (West Riding Regiment)

Titles:

1st Battalion

1702–1751	By the Colonel's name
1751–1782	The 33rd Regiment of Foot
1782–1853	The 33rd (1st York, West Riding) Regiment of Foot
1853–1881	The 33rd (Duke of Wellington's) Regiment

2nd Battalion

1787–1807	The 76th Regiment of Foot
1807–1812	The 76th (Hindoostan) Regiment of Foot
1812–1881	The 76th Regiment of Foot
1881–1920	The Duke of Wellington's (West Riding Regiment)
1920–	The Duke of Wellington's Regiment (West Riding)

Badges:

The Crest and Motto of the Duke of Wellington.
Authorised to the 33rd, 18 Jun 1853.
The Elephant with Howdah. Authorised to the 76th, 17 Jan 1807.

56 *2nd Lieutenant R E Maffett, Duke of Wellington's circa 1892*

Battle Honours:

(2)	HINDOOSTAN	20 Oct 1806		
(2)	PENINSULA	6 Apr 1815		
(1)	WATERLOO	8 Dec 1815		
(2)	SERINGAPATAM	28 May 1818		
(2)	NIVE	1 Jan 1845		
(1)	ALMA	16 Oct 1855		
(1)	INKERMAN	16 Oct 1855		
(1)	SEVASTOPOL	16 Oct 1855		

(1)	ABYSSINIA	21 Sep 1868		
(1)	DETTINGEN	11 Sep 1882		
(2)	ALLY GHUR	1 Oct 1886		
(2)	DELHI, 1803	1 Oct 1886		
(2)	LESWARREE	1 Oct 1886		
(2)	DEIG	1 Oct 1886		
(2)	MYSORE	12 Feb 1889		

Establishments, Strengths and Locations:

		Offrs	WOs	Sgts	Dmrs	R&F	Total
1st Bn	**Establishment**	24	2	39	16	720	801
	Strength	23	2	39	16	419	498
	Location	York (arrived Dec 1889)					
2nd Bn	**Establishment**	28	2	46	16	800	892
	Strength	25	2	43	16	794	880
	Location	Nova Scotia (arrived Sep 1888)					
Depot		Halifax (Yorkshire)					

Uniform

The Duke of Wellington's Regiment has a number of unusual distinctions. Of these the dignity of being named for, arguably, the most famous British General is the most striking. It is, besides, the only instance of the adoption for this purpose of the name of a person not a member of the Royal Family. The connection with the Duke was that he commanded the 33rd Foot at the end of the eighteenth century. By coincidence both the 33rd and the 76th had red facings; it was possibly not so much a coincidence that red was selected as it was the dominant colour in the Duke of Wellington's arms. At any rate, it was regarded by the Regiment as very important and its exchange for the ubiquitous English White in 1881 was greeted with dismay. Like others similarly deprived the Regiment fought hard for the return of its old colour, eventually winning the battle in March 1905.

In 1890, therefore, the Regiment looked at first glance much like many others and Simkin has drawn a familiar group. The CO on his charger wears what could be the medal for the Abyssinian campaign of 1867–68 and may well be based on a photograph of Lt Col Edward Nesbitt who served through it with the 33rd; in 1890 he was commanding the 2nd Bn in Canada. A general description of officers' dress appears elsewhere; details peculiar to the Regiment and illustrated by **Figs 56** and **57** are as follows. On the home service helmet was the universal plate with, in the centre, the crest of the Duke of Wellington in silver on a black velvet ground; the plate was not worn by the 2nd Bn on the white tropical helmet in Canada. Officers' collar badges were a pair of gilt elephants, facing inwards, with a silver howdah on their back – the badge unique to the 76th Foot. The same badge, but all in silver, appeared in

57 A Coy, 1st Bn Duke of Wellington's 1891 (Army Museums Ogilby Trust)

the centre of the gilt waistbelt clasp; the clasp worn by 2Lt Maffett in **Fig 56** is of course the universal pattern featuring the Royal Crest, as explained on page 48.

Simkin's drummer appears to be accurate except that he should not, according to the regulations, have worn the drum badge on the tunic sleeve. Various photographs of drummers up to about 1907 generally confirm that the badge was not in fact worn. The badge in the centre of the home service helmet plate was the crest of the Duke of Wellington in yellow metal within a circlet inscribed "WEST RIDING"; this centre was worn with a crown above, also in yellow metal, as the glengarry badge – see the drummer in the front row left of **Fig 57**. The collar badge was an elephant in yellow metal and this can be seen most clearly on the four men in the fourth and fifth rows left of **Fig 57** wearing the short-lived scarlet frock with facing colour shoulder straps. The Regimental title was embroidered in white on tunic shoulder straps on a slight curve "W.RIDING". Although it is difficult to be certain, it would appear that the fringes on the drummer's wings in **Fig 57** are threaded; by contrast (and it is precariously close to nit-picking to note this) Simkin's fringes are oddly stiffened rather than drawn in, and are also a little on the long side. Finally (and merely an observation!) the side-drum shown in **Fig 57** is evidently Ordnance issue and the shell is still plain brass; emblazoning was a matter for the Regiment to arrange if it wished and to pay for itself.

The Border Regiment

Titles:

1st Battalion

1702–1751	By the Colonel's name
1751–1782	The 34th Regiment of Foot
1782–1881	The 34th (Cumberland) Regiment of Foot

2nd Battalion

1756–1757	The 57th Regiment of Foot. Renumbered.
1757–1782	The 55th Regiment of Foot
1782–1881	The 55th (Westmoreland) Regiment of Foot

1881–1959	The Border Regiment

Amalgamation with the King's Own Royal Regiment (Lancaster)

1959–	The King's Own Royal Border Regiment

Battle Honours:

(1)	PENINSULA	29 Mar 1815
(1)	ALBUHERA	13 Jun 1817
(1)	VITTORIA	3 Jul 1817
(1)	PYRENEES	16 Aug 1823
(1)	NIVELLE	16 Aug 1823
(1)	NIVE	16 Aug 1823
(1)	ORTHES	16 Aug 1823
(2)	CHINA WITH THE DRAGON	12 Jan 1843
(1)	ARROYO DOS MOLINOS	30 May 1845
(2)	ALMA	16 Oct 1855
(2)	INKERMAN	16 Oct 1855
(1) (2)	SEVASTOPOL	16 Oct 1855
(1)	LUCKNOW	3 Sep 1863

Badges:

A Laurel Wreath. An old badge of the 34th said to be in memory of the battle of Fontenoy.

The Dragon superscribed "China". Authorised to the 55th, 12 Jan 1843.

A Maltese Cross Authorised 22 Jul 1881.

The Star of the Garter. Adopted from 1881. Originally the badge of the Westmoreland Militia.

The Red and White Tuft. Originally worn in the headdress by the 34th in memory of the battle of Arroyo dos Molinos. Shown on the helmet in the form of the red over white background to the plate.

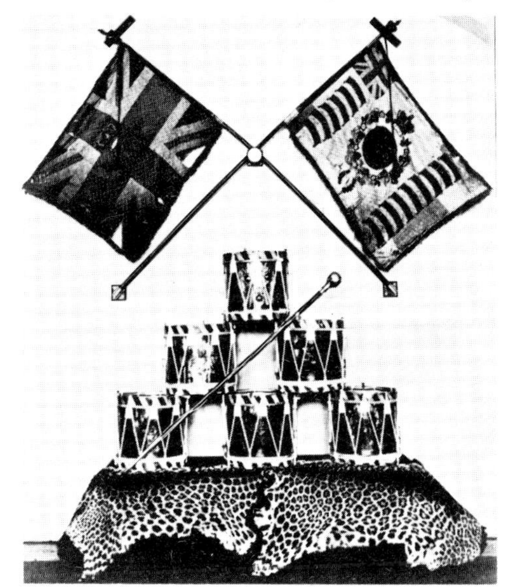

58 *The Colours of the 1st Bn, and the French Drums, of the Border Regiment photographed circa 1930*

Establishments, Strengths and Locations:

		Offrs	WOs	Sgts	Dmrs	R&F	Total
1st Bn	**Establishment**	28	2	45	16	920	1011
	Strength	27	2	39	10	781	859
	Location	Mandalay (arrived 1889)					
2nd Bn	**Establishment**	28	2	45	16	920	1011
	Strength	28	2	45	16	740	831
	Location	Chuckrata, Bengal (arrived Mar 1890)					
Depot		Carlisle					

Uniform

The Border Regiment is full of years and peculiar honours, pleasantly illustrated by Simkin's drawing. Besides a Sgt Dmr and a drummer, it shows the Colours of the 1st Bn and the French drums and Drum-Major's staff captured in the Peninsula. It was at the Battle of Arroyo dos Molinos on 28 October 1811 that the British 34th Foot defeated and captured the French 34th, complete with its corps of drums. These instruments have been a treasured trophy of the 1st Bn ever since and are shown in the photograph at **Fig 58**. The drums measure 16 inches in diameter and are 13½ inches deep; Simkin has illustrated them well. The shells are plain brass except that one has three brass grenades soldered on the front. The staff at just over 5 feet in length is the same size as its British equivalent but without any Regimental embellishments except for the title of the French Regiment engraved around the head.

Despite an extensive search, it has not been possible to find clear photographs of a Sgt Dmr and a drummer of the Regiment. However, both are to be seen, if rather indistinctly, in **Figs 59** and **60** which show the 2nd Bn on parade at Portsmouth on 6 October 1888 for the presentation of new Colours by the Duke of Cambridge. On the right of **Fig 60** the Sgt Dmr can be seen from his left rear standing next to a Bandsman. In **Fig 59**, between the Duke of Cambridge and the officer

60 *Officer, Bandsmen and Sergeant Drummer of 2nd Bn Border Regiment (same occasion as Fig 59) (Regimental Museum)*

59 *Presentation of New Colours to 2nd Bn Border Regiment by HRH Duke of Cambridge at Portsmouth on 6 Oct 1888 (Regimental Museum)*

carrying the Queen's Colour can be seen two drummers with a Bandsman between them. Not much is to be learned from such a poor photograph except that the drummers of the 2nd Bn, correctly, did not wear the drum badge on the tunic; Simkin has probably shown it in error. He may also have missed the apron but on the other hand we have no hard evidence one way or the other of its use by drummers of the 1st Bn.

Both men are shown correctly wearing the ORs' helmet with the usual embellishments and plate whose centre was an unusually large device featuring four of the Regiment's badges, all in white metal, a Maltese cross superimposed on a laurel wreath with, in the centre, a dragon; the lower part of the area behind the dragon was voided to show a backing of scarlet cloth *(19)*. The collar badge at this time was still the old pattern consisting of the China dragon embossed on a circular ground (in effect, a button) surrounded by a wreath, all in yellow metal. A change was made some years later to a Maltese cross surrounded by a wreath, in white metal. The shoulder straps were embroidered in a curve with "BORDER", in white for the Drummers and in gold for the Sgt Dmr. Finally, the latter's belt is correctly shown as the Ordnance issue pattern faced with white material and embroidered with the crowned Royal Cypher above the miniature drumsticks, and the Regimental title in gold on scrolls below.

The 1st Bn Colours have been represented quite accurately by Simkin. They were presented to the 34th Foot at Shorncliffe (Kent) by Lady Airey on 2 Aug 1871. Infantry Colours had been steadily reduced in size from 6ft 6in by 6ft 2in of the mid-eighteenth century and these were 3ft 9in by 3ft (on the pike) exclusive of the fringe which was about 2 inches deep. This size had been laid down in 1868 and is still valid today. The pike, however, was then 9ft 10in tall (including the gilt Royal Crest at the head), by comparison with the modern 8ft 7½in. Infantry battalions have carried two Colours for more than 200 years and they are known as the Queen's Colour, which for line infantry is basically the Union flag, and the Regimental Colour. The Queen's Colour was embellished, in 1871, with the number of the Regiment embroidered in Roman numerals with the crown above, all in gold (and colours). The Regimental Colour of the 34th was of yellow silk (the Regiment's facing colour) with a small Union in the upper canton. In the centre was the Union Wreath of Roses, Thistles and Shamrocks surmounted by a crown. Within that, on a scarlet ground, was a gold-edged circlet bearing the territorial title "CUMBERLAND", itself surrounding the Regimental number in gold Roman numerals – as on the Queen's Colour but smaller. At this point Simkin seems to have made a mistake as he has shown the Wreath (an ancient badge) around the number. This was in accordance with the regulations but not (see **Fig 58**) with fact for the wreath was actually embroidered (in green) at the bottom of the Colour below the central device. The artist was, however, entirely correct in his arrangement of the ten battle honours to which the 34th were entitled (see page 71). By the time the photograph at **Fig 58** was taken, more scrolls had been added to make a total of fifteen. By then, however, the Colours were in a poor state and no attempt was made to add the battle honours for the First World War to the Queen's Colour. Intended to last for twenty years, these Colours of the 34th should have been replaced in the 1890s but in fact continued in service until 1951, a remarkable innings of eighty years.

By way of a postscript, the 2nd Bn Colours shown in **Fig 59** were the same size and the Queen's Colour was of the same general design. The difference was that the central device was a gold-edged scarlet circlet bearing the title "THE BORDER REGIMENT", with a Roman two in the centre (for "2nd Bn") and a crown above. The Queen's Colour was quite different. Following the Regulations for Regiments with white facings, it was white with a (red) cross of St George. In the centre was the same device as the Regimental Colour, surrounded by the Union Wreath. Outside that a green laurel wreath was embroidered (on the white ground only) as a vehicle for the twelve battle honours (see page 71); the thirteenth, China, was embroidered with the dragon in the lower right corner and the wreath badge was placed in the lower left corner (or canton).

Finally, a post-postscript explains that the drum with the dog-tooth design in green and white on its hoops, to be seen in **Fig 59**, is a Russion one acquired on the field of Inkerman by Drummer Wainwright of the 55th Foot. It was carried for some years by the 2nd Bn The Border Regiment and may now be seen in the Regimental museum.

A Drummer-boy.

The Oxfordshire Light Infantry

Titles:

1st Battalion

1741–1748	By the Colonel's name
1748–1782	The 43rd Regiment of Foot
1782–1803	The 43rd (Monmouthshire) Regiment of Foot
1803–1881	The 43rd (Monmouthshire Light Infantry) Regiment

2nd Battalion

1755–1757	The 54th Regiment of Foot. Renumbered.
1757–1782	The 52nd Regiment of Foot
1782–1803	The 52nd (Oxfordshire) Regiment of Foot
1803–1881	The 52nd (Oxfordshire Light Infantry) Regiment
1881–1908	The Oxfordshire Light Infantry
1908–1958	The Oxfordshire and Buckinghamshire Light Infantry
1958–1966	The 1st Green Jackets, 43rd and 52nd

Absorbed into the Royal Green Jackets

1966–1968	The 1st Bn The Royal Green Jackets (43rd and 52nd)
1968–	The 1st Bn The Royal Green Jackets

Badges:

A Bugle-Horn. A badge of both the 43rd and the 52nd since conversion to Light Infantry in 1803.

The Rose. Given to the Regiment in 1881 in common with others which had no particular Regimental badge. Changed to the United Red and White Rose in 1888.

Battle Honours:

(1)(2) PENINSULA	
	6 Apr 1815(1/43,52) 1 Mar 1816 (2/43)
(2) WATERLOO	8 Dec 1815
(1)(2) VIMIERA	13 Feb 1821
(1)(2) BUSACO	13 Feb 1821
(1)(2) FUENTES D'ONOR	13 Feb 1821
(1)(2) CUIDAD RODRIGO	13 Feb 1821
(1)(2) BADAJOZ	13 Feb 1821
(1)(2) SALAMANCA	13 Feb 1821
(1)(2) VITTORIA	13 Feb 1821
(1)(2) NIVELLE	13 Feb 1821
(1)(2) NIVE	13 Feb 1821
(2) ORTHES	13 Feb 1821
(1)(2) TOULOUSE	13 Feb 1821
(1)(2) CORUNNA	
	20 Feb 1821(1/52) 8 Mar 1821(1/43)
(2) HINDOOSTAN	20 Feb 1821
(2) DELHI 1857	3 Sep 1863
(1) NEW ZEALAND	17 May 1870
(1) QUEBEC, 1759	13 March 1882
(1) SOUTH AFRICA, 1851–2–3	25 Jul 1882
(2) MYSORE	12 Feb 1889

61 *Captain C R Day, Oxfordshire Light Infantry, circa 1891 (Army Museums Ogilby Trust)*

Establishments, Strengths and Locations:

		Offrs	WOs	Sgts	Dmrs	R&F	Total
1st Bn	**Establishment**	24	2	39	16	720	801
	Strength	24	2	36	16	562	640
	Location	Portsmouth (arrived Jan 1890)					
2nd Bn	**Establishment**	28	2	45	16	920	1011
	Strength	28	2	41	15	969	1055
	Location	Toungoo, Burma (arrived Apr 1886)					
Depot		Oxford					

Uniform

One of the two Light Infantry Regiments illustrated in this volume, the Oxfordshire Light Infantry have the two most obvious distinctions of their class, green home service helmets and the stringed bugle horn badge. Simkin's officer shows both these; the bugle badge on the helmet plate is in silver on a black velvet ground, and it is illustrated in **Fig 61**. A less obvious Regimental distinction was the absence of a collar badge; for officers it was replaced by 2½ inches of gold russia braid running from the front of the collar to a small gilt button. This device was worn on the full dress tunic and on the scarlet patrol jacket (**Fig 62**). Other items of dress were in accordance with the regulations as described elsewhere.

Simkin has shown the soldiers of the Regiment in Field Day Order, i.e. in frocks and full dress headdress. The latter were as described elsewhere and the standard brass helmet plate had the stringed bugle device in the centre within a circlet inscribed "OXFORDSHIRE" all in brass. The seven-button frocks were the "second-tunic" kind with facings and badges as for the tunic itself and generally only lacking the white piping of the latter down the front and on the rear skirts – see **Fig 63**. There were no collar badges; before 1881 both the 43rd and 52nd had worn the stringed bugle but in Oct 1881 the new Regiment was authorised to dispense with them. Earlier that year, it received authority to wear the helmet plate centre as their glengarry

62 *Officers Oxfordshire Light Infantry in scarlet patrols circa 1893 (Army Museums Ogilby Trust)*

63 *Signallers 1st Bn Oxfordshire Light Infantry circa 1893 (Army Museums Ogilby Trust)*

badge but without the customary small crown above. This phenomenon can be seen in **Fig 63**. Also just discernible is the shape of the shoulder strap badge, consisting of a bugle horn above a curved "OXFORD", both embroidered in white on scarlet material. Buttons were of course in yellow metal and other badges were as laid down for all infantry.

In the centre of the group in **Fig 63** is the Assistant Instructor of Signalling of the 1st Bn about 1893. In addition to his sash, he wears three gold lace chevrons on his right arm with crossed signalling flags above. The other four men wear worsted badges of rank and good conduct of white on scarlet. Badges of qualification (crossed rifles for shooting; crossed flags for signalling) were embroidered in white and colours on scarlet – but see the book by Edwards and Langley *(24)* for details. The principal items of equipment to be seen are, first, the flags which came in pairs, one blue and one white with a central blue stripe; depending on the nature of the background against which he would be seen, the signaller used a dark or light coloured flag. There were also two sizes, 2 feet square and 3 feet square and it was reckoned that messages sent with the latter could be read in England at a range of 5–7 miles. Then in the centre, the Sergeant is operating a heliograph. This was a mirror mounted on a tripod and equipped with a sighting device and a key by which sunlight could be flashed directly at a required point. Messages were transmitted in Morse and in India ranges of up to 70 miles were achieved. The heliograph

was considered to be very effective as well as light and easy to carry; it did, however, demand the assistance of the sun and this must have been something of a limitation at home! Next, the Corporal, in the prone position, is using a telescope on a low tripod to read a message being transmitted to him at long range. Finally, the man on the right is to be seen recording the message in his "Army Signalling Message Book". But not shown in this photograph is the oil-lamp or limelight lamp used, with a shutter, for sending messages at night. The former, producing only a weak light, was used at ranges of up to 4 miles; the latter which produced a very bright light, could be read with a telescope at ranges in excess of 20 miles. But it was a rather complex piece of equipment requiring supplies of methylated spirits and of chemical agents from which the signaller had to generate his own requirements of oxygen. The oxygen gas bag on the ground with its rubber pipe up to the lamp on a tripod is an obvious feature by which this rather less than robust device can be recognised in old photographs.

Lastly, the reader may note that the men in **Fig 63** are wearing the 1882 pattern belt. The 1st Bn was issued with the Lee-Metford rifle in Apr 1892 and in Sep of that year with the 1888 pattern pouches. However, it was not until 1895 that the full Slade-Wallace equipment was provided. Meanwhile the 2nd Bn in India received their Lee-Metfords in late 1893 and their new equipment probably some years later.

The Northamptonshire Regiment

Titles:

1st Battalion

1741–1751	By the Colonel's name
1751–1782	The 48th Regiment of Foot
1782–1881	The 48th (Northamptonshire) Regiment of Foot

2nd Battalion

1755–1757	The 60th Regiment of Foot. Renumbered.
1757–1782	The 58th Regiment of Foot
1782–1881	The 58th (Rutlandshire) Regiment of Foot

1881–1960	The Northamptonshire Regiment

Amalgamation with the Lincolnshire Regiment

1960–1964	The 2nd East Anglian Regiment (Duchess of Gloucester's Own Royal Lincolnshire and Northamptonshire)

Absorbed into The Royal Anglian Regiment

1964–1968	The 2nd (Duchess of Gloucester's Own Lincolnshire and Northamptonshire) Battalion, The Royal Anglian Regiment
1968–	The 2nd Battalion (Lincolnshire, Leicestershire and Northamptonshire) The Royal Anglian Regiment

Battle Honours:

(1) (2) LOUISBURG	
(1) (2) QUEBEC 1759	
(2) GIBRALTAR with the Castle, Key and "Montis Insignia Calpe'	22 Apr 1784
(2) EGYPT AND THE SPHINX	6 Jul 1802
(2) MAIDA	12 Feb 1807
(1) (2) PENINSULA	6 Apr 1815
(1) TALAVERA	6 Nov 1816
(1) DOURO	22 Jan 1818
(1) ALBUHERA	22 Jan 1818
(1) BADAJOZ	22 Jan 1818
(1) (2) SALAMANCA	22 Jan 1818 (1/48) 14 Feb 1821 (2/58)
(1) (2) VITTORIA	22 Jan 1818 (1/48) 1 Feb 1821 (2/58)
(1) (2) PYRENEES	22 Jan 1818 (1/48) 14 Feb 1821 (2/58)
(1) (2) NIVELLE	22 Jan 1818 (1/48) 14 Feb 1821 (2/58)
(1) (2) ORTHES	22 Jan 1818 (1/48) 14 Feb 1821 (2/58)
(1) TOULOUSE	22 Jan 1818
(1) SEVASTOPOL	16 Oct 1855
(2) NEW ZEALAND	17 May 1870
(2) SOUTH AFRICA, 1879	25 Jul 1882

Badges:

The Castle, Key and Motto "Montis Insignia Calpe". Authorised to the 58th, 2 May 1836, but adopted before.

The Sphinx superscribed "Egypt". Authorised to the 58th, 6 Jul 1802.

A Golden Horseshoe. The old badge of the Rutland Militia which was added to the Regular battalions' badges in 1881.

Establishments, Strengths and Locations:

		Offrs	WOs	Sgts	Dmrs	R&F	Total
1st Bn	**Establishment**	24	2	39	16	720	801
	Strength	23	2	37	16	528	606
	Location	Warley (arrived Mar 1888)					
2nd Bn	**Establishment**	28	2	46	16	920	1012
	Strength	28	2	37	14	932	1013
	Location	Straits Settlements (arrived Jan 1889)					
Depot		Northampton					

Uniform

This is a splendid "Simkin" showing, evidently, the Commanding Officer of a Battalion of the Regiment in a fine commanding stance. With him is his Bugler, the counterpart of today's radio operator. In the background are men of the Battalion. All ranks are in Review Order and perhaps on their way to a grand parade in Aldershot where the 1st Bn were stationed for a while from late 1890. The only problem is that neither 1st nor 2nd Bn at this time wore the blue home service helmet; the 2nd Bn in the Straits Settlements would have been wearing the foreign pattern white helmet of the day, while the 1st had received the trial universal white helmet (see **Fig 82**) in the early summer of 1889. **Fig 64** dates from circa 1888 and has been deliberately chosen to complement Simkin's drawing.

The CO, a Lieutenant Colonel, is shown in accordance with the regulations, and there is no reason to believe that practice was any different. The gilt helmet plate incorporated *(10)* a central device of the Castle and Key with a scroll above inscribed "GIBRALTAR" and another below inscribed "TALAVERA", all in silver on a black velvet ground. The collar badges were complex: a gilt wreath surrounded a gilt circle pierced "NORTHAMPTONSHIRE REGT" on a blue enamel ground; within the circle on a blue enamel ground, a silver cross of St George; on the circle a silver horseshoe and above the circle a crown in gilt (see Dress Regulations 1883 and 1891). Other details were as described on page 48; see also page 24.

The only photograph of an officer of the period in full dress that the author was able to find is rather small for our purpose (**Fig 64**) but there are compensations. It is one of a number taken when the 1st Bn did duty at the Tower of London and shows a Guard of Honour formed up awaiting a dignitary. On the left of the group, under the arch, are two men off duty in glengarries and frocks; behind them are two others less smartly turned out. Then there is the sentry, looking at the camera. Next, two Sgts, and then the men of the Guard. Confusingly in a Regiment which did not serve in the Egyptian campaign, no less than six men can be seen wearing the medals, notably the Khedive's Star; they presumably transferred from another Regiment. This probability seems to be confirmed by another photograph taken about the same time which shows a group of Sgts who are undeniably of the 1st Bn including one man who is wearing two Egyptian Medals. **Fig 64** shows the Martini Henry and triangular bayonet to good effect; it also includes a Yeoman Warder in his blue and scarlet undress uniform.

Simkin's Drummer is correctly drawn as proved by **Fig 65**. This photograph was taken at the Tower of London in the summer of 1889 or 1890 and illustrates the following points: the other ranks blue glengarry worn, as here perhaps, when not on a formal parade and complete with the crowned brass helmet plate centre (as for officers with the Castle and Key and scrolls for "GIBRALTAR" and "TALAVERA" within a circlet inscribed "NORTHAMPTONSHIRE") as badge, tunics laced according to regulation as described elsewhere; brass collar badge of a cross within a circlet inscribed "NORTHAMPTONSHIRE", the whole surmounted by a crown; the title "NORTHAMPTON" embroidered on each shoulder strap in white in a curve amounting almost to a semicircle; drum badge not worn on the tunic (though, from another photograph, we know it was worn on the frock); green bugle cords so arranged that the tassels are at the left shoulder; apron; the odd variety of drum carriages and the unusual, even awkward, height at which No 3 from the left has fitted his drum; finally, the emblazoning on the drums.

Behind the Drummers in **Fig 65** is the Sgt Dmr in his SSgt's forage cap of blue with a black band and gold embroidered badge; his tunic is according to the description on page 47 and

64 *Guard of 1st Bn Northamptonshire Regiment circa 1888 (Army Museums Ogilby Trust)*

65 *Drummers 1st Bn Northamptonshire Regiment, Tower of London circa 1890 (Army Museums Ogilby Trust)*

the interesting features are therefore his belt and staff or mace. The belt is thought to have been faced with buff felt and edged with gold lace; the embellishments were possibly embroidered in silver on velvet of a darker colour than buff. The staff of which only the head survives in the Regimental Museum was apparently at least 6 feet tall; the head is 16 inches tall, the crown occupying the top 3 inches, and is 5 inches in diameter at its broadest. It is of yellow metal with white metal embellishments: fourteen battle honour scrolls on an oak wreath forming the upper ring, and eight-pointed stars on either side. One of these has in the centre the figure "48" surrounded by a circlet with "NORTHAMPTONSHIRE REGIMENT" on it; the other has the cypher "VR" with a garter and "HONI SOIT QVI MAL Y PENSE". One of the "battle honour" scrolls proclaims that the staff was presented by Major W H Knight in 1870.

Finally, **Fig 66** is an amusing vignette fairly obviously posed for the photographer: the Sergeant Major on the left looks particularly uncomfortable though neither man seems very happy – with the photographer or the beer? Both wear the same tunic with ½-inch gold braid on the collar and cuffs. The Sergeant Major has scarlet shoulder straps, edged with gold russia braid and with the Regimental title embroidered in gold; his badge is a crown. The Bandmaster has gold ("engineer" pattern – i.e. with a trefoil at the end) shoulder cords and the distinctive badge of his appointment, a crowned lyre with a sprig of oakleaves on either side at the base, embroidered in gold on his right forearm. (Bandsmen at that time wore a crowned harp on crossed trumpets embroidered in white.) Both Warrant Officers wear officers' pattern forage caps.

66 *Sergeant Major and Bandmaster 1st Bn Northamptonshire Regiment circa 1890 (Army Museums Ogilby Trust)*

The Duke of Edinburgh's (Wiltshire Regiment)

Titles:

1st Battalion

1756–1758	2nd Battalion the 4th (King's Own) Regiment of Foot. Separately constituted as the 62nd Foot
1758–1782	The 62nd Regiment of Foot
1782–1881	The 62nd (The Wiltshire) Regiment of Foot

2nd Battalion

1824–1874	The 99th (Lanarkshire) Regiment of Foot
1874–1881	The 99th (The Duke of Edinburgh's) Regiment of Foot
1881–1920	The Duke of Edinburgh's (Wiltshire Regiment)
1920–1959	The Wiltshire Regiment (Duke of Edinburgh's)

Amalgamation with The Royal Berkshire Regiment

1959–	The Duke of Edinburgh's Royal Regiment (Berkshire and Wiltshire)

67 *Lieutenant, Wiltshire Regiment circa 1886 (Regimental Museum)*

Badges:

The Duke of Edinburgh's Coronet and Cypher. Authorised, with the title, to the 99th, 22 Apr 1874.

A Maltese Cross. Said to have been adopted by the 62nd in 1806.

Battle Honours:

(1) PENINSULA	26 May 1829	(1) SEVASTOPOL	16 Oct 1855
(1) NIVE	1 Feb 1844	(2) PEKIN	4 Nov 1861
(1) FEROZESHAH	8 Jun 1847	(2) NEW ZEALAND	17 May 1870
(1) SOBRAON	8 Jun 1847	(2) SOUTH AFRICA, 1879	25 Jul 1882

Establishments, Strengths and Locations:

		Offrs	WOs	Sgts	Dmrs	R&F	Total
1st Bn	Establishment	24	2	39	16	720	801
	Strength	23	2	38	15	742	820
	Location	Athlone (arrived Aug 1887)					
2nd Bn	Establishment	28	2	45	16	920	1011
	Strength	28	2	44	16	984	1074
	Location	Meean Meer, Bengal (arrived Jan 1882)					
Depot		Devizes					

Uniform

Unfortunately Devizes Railway Station is now disused and closed but the author understands that Simkin's impression of it is very fair. Certainly, it must have been a familiar spot for thousands of soldiers of the 90s on their way to or from the manoeuvres and garrisons in the area. But for the Wiltshires, it was the home stop: their depot was just up the road.

The officer is wearing his full dress headdress, illustrated in **Fig 67**. The badge is the gilt universal crowned star with, in the centre, a gilt Maltese cross on a black velvet ground; in the middle of the Maltese cross, the Duke of Edinburgh's coronet and cypher in silver; on the silver scroll below the centre, "THE WILTSHIRE REGT". The patrol jacket was as described on page 50 and illustrated in **Fig 68**. The collar badge was common to it and the tunic, and consisted of a silver Maltese cross with the coronet and cypher in gilt: the reverse in short of the device on the helmet plate. The round forage cap to be seen in **Fig 68** was dark blue with a black lace band and, for officers of the 1st Bn – also of the 3rd (Militia) Bn – a metal badge consisting of a gilt Maltese cross with coronet above, the coronet and cypher in silver in the centre and a gilt scroll below proclaiming "THE WILTSHIRE REGT". A metal badge was unusual and the 2nd Bn was in step with most of the rest of the Infantry in wearing an embroidered one: the Maltese cross and coronet in gold; in the centre of the cross on a ground of blue velvet, the cypher in silver with the coronet above it in gold; below the cross a light blue silk label embroidered in gold with the Regimental title. The waistbelt plate was as usual gilt, with, in the centre, the badge in silver and gilt as on the collar.

The soldiers in Simkin's drawing are dressed as described elsewhere in full dress helmet, frock and 1888 pattern equipment. The helmet plate centre consisted of the Maltese cross with coronet and cypher, all in brass. The collar badge was, similarly, a brass Maltese cross, and the shoulder title was "WILTS" worked in white embroidery on scarlet (or scarlet embroidery on white on the short-lived scarlet frock which

68 *Officers 1st Bn Wiltshire Regiment, Aldershot 1895 (Regimental Museum)*

69 *1st Bn Wiltshire Regiment on manoeuvres 1893 (Regimental Museum)*

70 Foot Inspection – 1st Bn Wiltshire Regiment 1893 (Regimental Museum)

displayed the facing colour on the shoulder straps only; some can be seen in **Figs 69** and **70**). Points to note in Simkin's drawing are the CSgt's badge, correctly in undress a crown over three chevrons; the spare magazine pouch worn by the right-hand seated man and the white painted title "2 WILTS" on the back of the valise.

Finally, the author apologises for the poor quality of **Figs 69** and **70** but they have been included because they are typical of the sights to be seen in Hampshire and Wiltshire late every summer through the 1890s. The battalion on the march might usually have been headed by the Pioneers but **Fig 69** is a conundrum: only one pouch on each of the eight men in the front of the Band, no Pioneers' badge and no tools. The likely solution is that they are Signallers. The evidence that Pioneers' badges were worn by the Wiltshires stands in line third from right in **Fig 70**. Here the officers have evidently found some particularly interesting feet (on the left) while the remainder of the squad waits for theirs to be checked after the day's march. Foot inspections, like rifle inspections, have for many years been carried out simply to ensure that the soldier looks after his most important equipment; to some officers, it is a constant source of surprise that he does not.

The Durham Light Infantry

Titles:

1st Battalion

1756–1758	2nd Bn 23rd Royal Welsh Fusiliers. Reformed.
1758–1782	The 68th Regiment of Foot
1782–1808	The 68th (Durham) Regiment of Foot
1808–1881	The 68th (Durham Light Infantry) Regiment

2nd Battalion

1826–1840	The Hon East India Company's 2nd Bombay European Regiment
1840–1858	The 2nd Bombay European Light Infantry
1858–1861	The 2nd Bombay Light Infantry Regiment
1861–1881	The 106th (Bombay Light Infantry) Regiment
1881–1968	The Durham Light Infantry

Amalgamation with the King's Own Yorkshire Light Infantry, The Somerset and Cornwall Light Infantry, and the King's Shropshire Light Infantry

1968–	The Light Infantry

Badges:

A Light Infantry Bugle Horn. Adopted in 1808 by the 68th when the Regiment was made Light Infantry.
A French Bugle Horn. A badge of the 106th.
The Rose. Given to the Regiment in 1881 in common with others which had no particular Regimental badge. Changed to the United Red and White Rose in 1888.

71 *Lieutenant F H S Sitwell, Durham Light Infantry circa 1885 (Regimental Museum)*

Battle Honours:

(1) PENINSULA	6 Apr 1815	(1) INKERMAN	16 Oct 1855
(1) SALAMANCA	20 Jun 1823	(1) SEVASTOPOL	16 Oct 1855
(1) PYRENEES	20 Jun 1823	(2) PERSIA	GGO 332/1861
(1) VITTORIA	20 Jun 1823	(2) RESHIRE	GGO 332/1861
(1) NIVELLE	20 Jun 1823	(2) BUSHIRE	GGO 332/1861
(1) ORTHES	20 Jun 1823	(2) KOOSHAB	GGO 332/1861
(1) ALMA	16 Oct 1855	(1) NEW ZEALAND	17 May 1870

Establishments, Strengths and Locations:

		Offrs	WOs	Sgts	Dmrs	R&F	Total
1st Bn	**Establishment**	24	2	39	16	720	801
	Strength	25	2	37	16	617	697
	Location	Bradford (arrived May 1889)					
2nd Bn	**Establishment**	28	2	45	16	920	1011
	Strength	26	2	44	16	962	1060
	Location	Poona, Bengal (arrived Jan 1887)					
Depot		Newcastle-on-Tyne					

Uniform

This coloured plate seems to be one of Simkin's less imaginative compositions but it does in fact illustrate a regulation movement. Even so, the author defies anyone to run very far with a rifle at the slope! At the time it was published, the print from this drawing was clearly an inspiration to the model soldier makers, Messrs Wm Britain & Co. The drawing also reminds us that its subject is a Light Infantry Regiment. Expected historically to move more quickly than heavy infantry, the conversion of the 1st Bn was approved by King George III in 1808. The letter from the Duke of York, as Commander-in-Chief, to the Secretary at War illustrates the differences at the time:

"Horse Guards. 10 September, 1808.

Sir,

His Majesty having taken into His Consideration that the Proportion of Light Troops was much too small for the extended Scale of the British Army and that the utility of this Description of Force had been most eminently displayed on every occasion when they have been employed, and the whole of that Army being at this moment embarked or employed upon Foreign Service, I have to acquaint you that His Majesty has been pleased to command that two more Battalions of the Line should be formed into Light Troops with all practicable Dispatch, and that the 68th and 85th Regiments should be allotted for this purpose, and assimilated with regard to their Clothing, Arming, and Discipline to the 43rd and 52nd Regiments, and that in consequence thereof, an additional Lieutenant, Serjeant and Corporal per Company be borne on the Establishment of the 68th and 85th Regiments; You will therefore give the necessary Directions accordingly.

I am, Sir,

Yours,

Frederick, Commander-in-Chief"

By 1890, as we have noted elsewhere, differences between Light Infantry and the remainder of the Line had disappeared except in the area of dress and appointments.

All ranks are shown wearing the full dress headdress, as was correct in Field Day Order. The jacket was the scarlet patrol for the officer, and seven-button frock for other ranks. The men wear the 1888 pattern waistbelt and the right pouch only, together with the haversack and the water-bottle, and they carry the Lee-Metford rifle. It is interesting to compare this with an account preserved in the Regimental records of the

72 *Officers 1st Bn Durham Light Infantry circa 1892 (Regimental Museum)*

dress and equipment of the 1st Bn on the Aldershot Manoeuvres of 1893. They wore what was referred to as Light Service Order consisting of: full dress headdress, frock, trousers, boots and leggings, two pouches, haversack and water-bottle; they also had the cape rolled and the greatcoat rolled but did not have (curiously) the waterproof sheet. Light Service Order was actually Service Marching Order but without the valise. It therefore included the braces and, although it

73 *K Coy 1st Bn Durham Light Infantry, India circa 1885 (Regimental Museum)*

is not mentioned in the record, the mess-tin. The tail ends of the braces were passed through the outer (of 3) buckles at the rear of the belt, around the greatcoat (tightly rolled 15in long) and then back through the buckles; spare lengths of brace after that were neatly coiled against the buckle. The cape was rolled similarly and secured behind the shoulders by means of the valise equipment greatcoat straps, which were fastened around the cape, passed forward on top of the braces, through the "D"s, under the shoulder straps and buckled to the double buckles above the pouches. The mess-tin was secured by its own strap above the rolled greatcoat to the centre buckle at the rear of the waistbelt. Finally, the 1st Bn had the Lee-Metford having been issued in the spring of 1891; the 2nd Bn received the new rifle at Mhow in India two years later.

Simkin's officer wears the green, Light Infantry pattern, helmet with gilt fittings. This is illustrated in **Fig 71**; the centre of the badge consisted of a silver stringed bugle on the black velvet ground, and on the silver scroll below was "THE DURHAM LIGHT INFANTRY". The collar badges worn on the tunic and on the scarlet patrol jacket illustrated in **Fig 72** were the same: gold embroidered stringed bugles worn as a pair, bells outermost. The centre of the gilt waistbelt clasp was, like the helmet plate, a silver stringed bugle. **Fig 72** also illustrates the variety of forage or undress caps worn by officers. The round peaked cap was dark green with a black band and the stringed bugle badge embroidered in gold had in the centre (scarcely visible in the photograph) the letters "DLI"

embroidered in gold on a blue ground. In **Fig 73**, the two officers wear the previous and rather more squat pattern of this cap, though with the same badge. Finally, in **Fig 72**, two officers wear a green Torin cap with a green corded boss, bearing a very small silver stringed bugle, on the front.

Other ranks wore the Light Infantry pattern green helmet with, in the centre of the universal brass plate, a brass stringed bugle. This central device complete with circlet was used as the glengarry badge, without a separate crown (see **Fig 73**). The collar badges were brass stringed bugles worn in pairs, bells pointing outwards, as for officers. The shoulder titles consisted of the word "DURHAM" embroidered in a curve with a bugle horn above, all in white. Three other features are worth noting, at least on the evidence of **Fig 73**; the buglers have not run strings through the fringes of their wings and, contrary to the regulations, they are wearing the white embroidered bugle badge on the tunic. Behind them the two Sergeants have a silver whistle and chain attached to a boss which seems to have been pinned or "plugged" into the tunic. From other photographs, it is deduced that the 1st Bn had abandoned this custom by 1899 but it was still maintained by the 2nd Bn in that year. This was a feature of the pre-Crimea uniform of all Light Infantry Sergeants. It was retained in the case of the 68th as a reminder of the Battle of Inkerman in which the Regiment suffered heavy officer casualties; it may also have been to recall the fact that the Regiment reputedly threw off its greatcoats and was the only one to fight that day in red jackets.

THE SCOTTISH LINE

General Introduction

Naturally enough, there have been soldiers in Scotland for centuries. Indeed for much of the time they were a major export business as well. But it was not until 1739 that they were first enlisted in the British standing Army wearing their native garb. Since then, while remaining undoubtedly characteristic, the dress of Scottish Regiments had been much simplified. To some extent it had also been stylised under the pressure on the one hand of Victorian romanticism, which imposed its own view of what the tradition should be, and on the other hand of modern living; this forced out, for example, early in the last century the kilt-and-plaid-in-one which reputedly could only be put on by lying on the ground and rolling oneself into it. A description of the various items of military Scottish dress at the time with which we are concerned may therefore serve as a useful introduction to the three Regiments featured in this section.

Full Dress Headdress

Lowland Regiments and the Scottish Rifles wore the common home service helmet, except the Royal Scots Fusiliers who wore of course the fusilier cap. With the exception of the Highland Light Infantry in their shakos, all the Highland Regiments wore the feather bonnet (see **Fig 75**). This had spent some years developing from a knitted cap with a feather stuck in it to the eventual wire frame with a knitted diced band and a complete covering of ostrich feathers, including a number of so-called "fox tails". For officers it was eventually laid down in Dress Regulations 1900 that these should be of different numbers by Regiments (Black Watch: 4; Seaforth, Gordon and Cameron Highlanders: 5; Argylls: 6) and it is likely that this served merely to confirm accepted Regimental practice. For ORs, however, the scene is not so clear. No sealed patterns seem to have survived from the 1880s and detailed records of

74 *Highland Doublet*

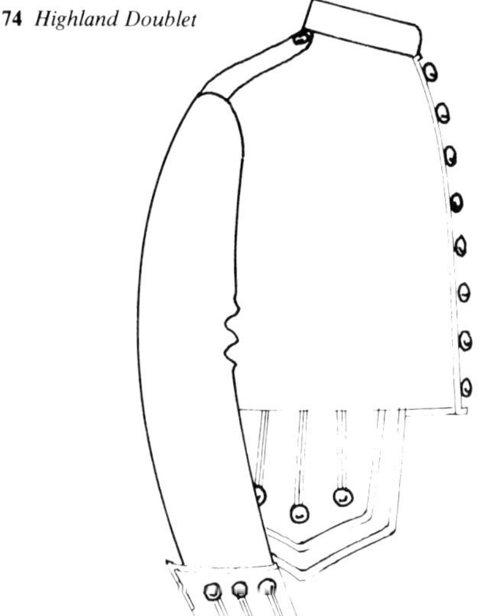

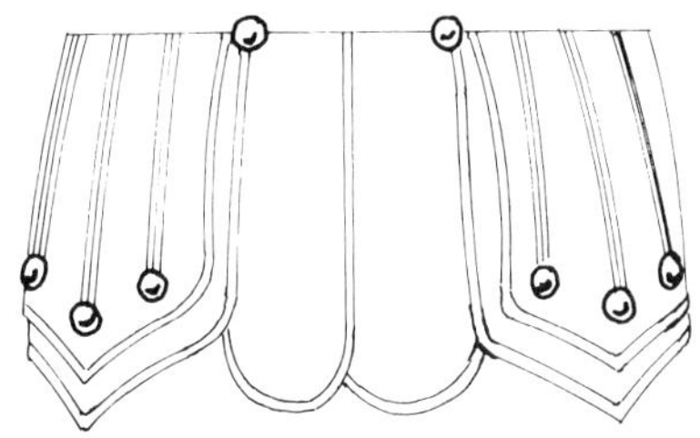

a *and* **b** *Other Ranks*

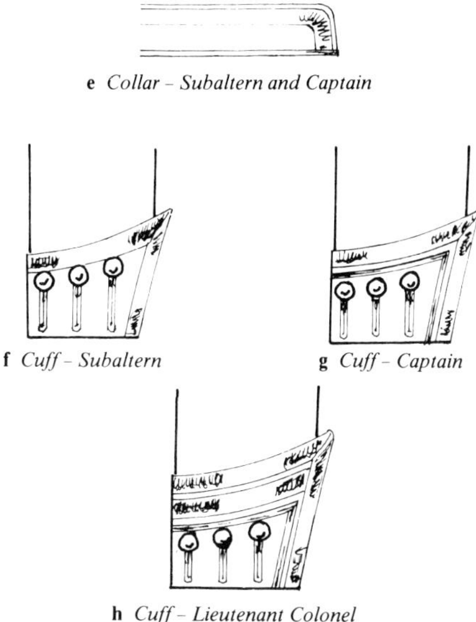

e *Collar – Subaltern and Captain*

f *Cuff – Subaltern*

g *Cuff – Captain*

h *Cuff – Lieutenant Colonel*

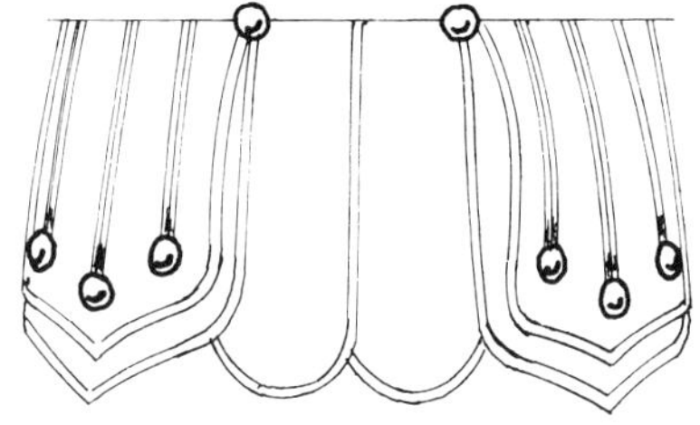

j *Skirts – Subaltern and Captain*

the day are by no means complete. But they do show that a bonnet with four tails of equal length was adopted in May 1886 as a sealed pattern for ORs of all Regiments. With no evidence to the contrary, it seems likely that this was what was worn in 1890. Still it is worth noting that the decision by the War Office over-ruled appeals by the Argylls and the Camerons to be allowed to retain their own pattern bonnet with five tails and by 2nd Bn The Gordon Highlanders to have their four tails in graduated lengths, the longest at the rear; such bonnets may still have been in use in 1890 not least because the headdress was expected to last twelve years before replacement. It is also worth noting that the demand for standardisation was driven as ever by economy and it was War Office policy that bonnets should pass from Regiment to Regiment as battalions went on or returned from foreign service. Thus the 1st Black Watch were required to hand theirs over to 2nd Gordons in 1882. This would have required changes of diced band (red, white and blue for Royal Regiments and red, white and green for others, except the Argylls who had red and white) and of cap badge

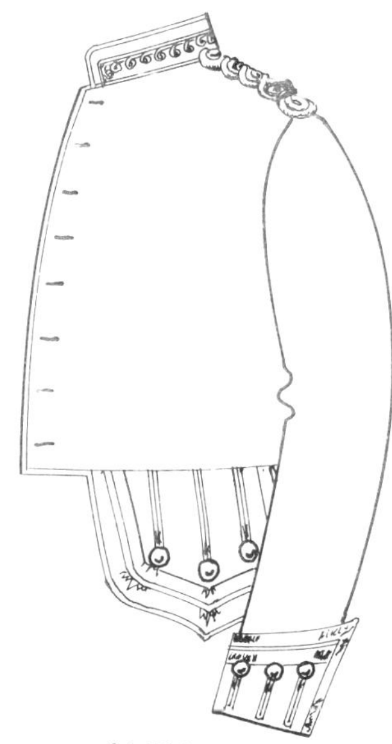

c and d *Major*

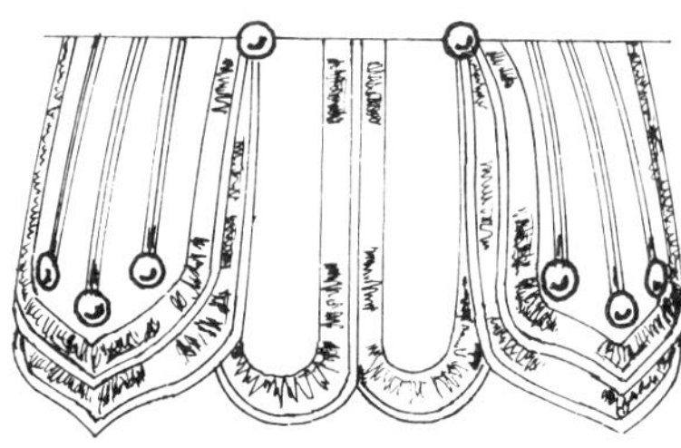

74 *Highland Doublet*

(also of hackle where the Black Watch were concerned; they alone wore a scarlet one). The pattern allowed for such changes. On the other hand the black cocade (leather for R&F and silk for Staff Sergeants and Officers) was standard as were the black ribbons which fell to about the level of the collar at the rear.

Full Dress Doublet
The doublet (for all Regiments except the Scottish Rifles) was a single-breasted scarlet jacket (see **Fig 74**) with a stand collar like a tunic, and shoulder straps which were of the same design. The front was edged white from collar to waist. Below the waist were so-called "Inverness skirts" 6½ inches deep; these consisted of four large and, in the centre of the rear, two small flaps. All the flaps were lined and edged with white cloth. The four larger ones had false pocket-flaps, also edged white, on top; each of these secured with three buttons at the foot of a length of braid. The cuffs were the so-called "gauntlet" type and rose from 4 inches deep in front to about 6 inches in rear. Like the pocket-flaps, each cuff was edged with white cloth and secured with three buttons on a length of braid.

The Kilt and Plaid
The Highland soldier was originally dressed in the belted plaid (or *breacan an fheilidh*) of his countrymen. It consisted of 12 ells (1 ell = 45 inches) of doubled material and was belted at the waist and buttoned or tied at the shoulder to form the kilt-and-plaid-in-one. By about 1814 it had been superseded by the "little kilt" (or *feile-beag*). This is essentially still the same today and consists of 6 ells of single material, pleated and sewn down at the waist except for ½ell at either end; this is left unpleated and is crossed over to give a flat appearance in front. With the kilt, in 1890, some ranks and appointments wore a separate plaid in one of three forms. The most voluminous was the scarf or modified shoulder plaid which was folded in a particular manner, passed around the body under the right arm, fastened at the left shoulder with a brooch in a particular Regimental or even battalion manner, and then allowed to fall about the left arm. The other two forms were versions of the late nineteenth-century belted plaid sometimes called a "fly"; this was a piece of tartan material pleated and stitched to a belt or tape which was fastened round the waist under the doublet. The part which then trailed down behind was lifted and, in the first version, a small piece of tartan attached to it passed under the left shoulder strap to represent the front fall of the plaid. Often untraditionally fringed, this plaid was fastened at the left shoulder with a brooch (see **Fig 75** – The Sgts of the Seaforths and Gordons). In the second version, the trailing corner of the material had a little rosette and green tape which was lifted up and secured to the left shoulder strap button (see **Fig 76**).

The Sporran
What is commonly called a "sporran", or more properly a purse, supplies the function of the pocket for small articles noticeably missing from traditional Highland clothing. In the Army of 1890, this functional container was obscured by a large confection of Regimental design weighing anything up to 2lb. It was secured by a leather strap which was passed around the body some inches below the waist through tape loops attached to the kilt.

75 *Sergeants of Highland Regiments 1888. Left to right: Black Watch, Highland Light Infantry, Seaforths, Camerons, Gordons, Argyll and Sutherland Highlanders*

Hose, Garters and Spats

The tartan hose were originally pieces of tartan material cut to shape and seamed up the back of the leg. Because they were without elasticity, they needed to be kept up and the means of this was a scarlet garter traditionally about 3 feet long, wound around the leg and secured with a special knot. By 1890, the military version of the hose was knitted but the garter was retained, usually to be observed in the form of a "flash" showing below the hose cuff. The spats had their origin in the functional short grey gaiters worn by all British infantry in the Peninsula. By 1890 they had become white and larger; they had also acquired whalebone stiffeners up the back of the leg. They were made of canvas, strapped under foot, and fastened on the outside with, usually, white bone buttons.

Trews

Tartan trousers, called trews, were worn in all orders of dress by officers and men of Lowland Regiments and in certain orders of dress only by Highlanders. There were also tartan overalls (or tight trousers) and breeches worn with knee boots by mounted officers. The tartan, as for the kilt and plaid, was of Regimental pattern.

Weapons

The personal weapons carried by Highland officers and soldiers (broadsword or claymore, dirk and skean dhu) are described briefly on page 19.

Other Ranks Full Dress

The junior rank of the Scottish Regiment in full dress wore his Regimental headdress. All, less the Scottish Rifles and all pipers, wore a scarlet doublet as described above with collar and cuffs in the Regimental facing colour. All piping and braid on the scarlet doublet was white. The shoulder straps, secured with a small brass button, were scarlet and were embroidered in white with an abbreviated version of the Regimental title. Good conduct badges were of $\frac{1}{2}$-inch white braid on scarlet worn, as for other infantry, point uppermost on the left fore-arm. Valise equipment and weapons were as described elsewhere and all other items of dress were of Regimental pattern.

Sergeant's Class Doublet

As for other infantry, a Sergeant's doublet was of better quality material than for junior ranks. Badges of rank were as described on page 45). There were no other special embellishments apart from the customary red sash.

Staff Sergeant's Class Doublet

Also as for other infantry, a Staff Sergeant's doublet was again of better quality material. It was laced along the top and front of the collar with ½-inch gold lace and along the base of the collar with ⅛-inch gold russia braid. The cuffs were edged along the top and rear with ½-inch gold lace and the button-holes on the cuffs and pocket flaps were made of gold russia braid. As for other infantry, the shoulder straps were edged with gold russia braid and the Regimental title was embroidered in gold. This pattern doublet was worn by Warrant Officers and Staff Sergeants as defined elsewhere.

Other Dress Distinctions

In most Scottish Regiments (aside of course from the Rifles) the WOs wore an officer's sash (see **Fig 80**), some even wearing it like an officer over the left shoulder (see **Fig 83**). SSgts and Sgts wore the more usual variety. WOs also generally carried an officer's broadsword and it was not unknown for them to wear officer's patterns of belts, sporran, dirk, shoulder belt plate, plaid brooch and other tribal items. Further reference to such characteristics is made in the Regimental sections that follow.

Drummers

The principal difference in full dress of a drummer lay in the lacing of his doublet. Basically the same as that of a private, it had "crown and inch" lace (see page 46) along the top and front of the collar, down the front and rear seams of each sleeve, and on all the seams on the back above the waist (see **Fig 77**); secondly the button loops on the Inverness skirts and on the cuffs were made of red and white worsted braid. The wings were of the same pattern as Line Infantry, but without a fringe. There are two other points to note: in Lowland Regiments with trews aprons were sometimes worn, while in Highland Regiments a kilted drummer often either wore no sporran or pushed it around to the side or rear.

Pipers

By 1890, Scots Guards and Highland Regiment battalions were each established for a Sergeant Piper and five pipers in addition to a Sergeant Drummer and the customary sixteen drummers. In most cases, however, there were at least twelve and often more pipers in a battalion, the majority being "unofficial". In Lowland Regiments, all pipers were "unofficial". No piper wore a feather bonnet at this time but instead a glengarry of Regimental pattern. All except those of the Scots Guards wore a dark green doublet. These had no facings but were braided and laced in white or silver generally in the same manner as the other rank's scarlet doublet. (Pipers of the Argylls at this time had white piping, like bandsmen, on the back of the sleeves and down the back of the doublet; it is not thought that other Regiments shared this practice.) The kilt and shoulder plaid were often of a different tartan from that worn by the remainder of the Regiment, while the sporran, plaid brooch and personal arms (dirk and skean dhu) were usually of special pipers' patterns. But several items were quite different:

Dirk-belt or Waistbelt: This was always of black (possibly patent) leather and fastened in front with a large clasp of

76 *Sergeant Argyll and Sutherland Highlanders circa 1891 (Army Museums Ogilby Trust)*

Regimental design. Its only function was to support the dirk worn just forward of the right hip (see **Fig 81**).

Baldrick or Shoulder Belt: This too was of black (patent) leather embellished with a large buckle, slide and tip of Regimental design on the front; in some Regiments there was also a badge or other device. The baldrick was the ceremonial version of the ancient sword belt, with a frog at the lower end on the left hip. On occasions the Sergeant Piper of a battalion wore a broadsword on this belt but for most pipers it was merely an ornamental item of kit without practical function.

The Pipes: These, and their music, are a subject all on their own. But for the layman it is enough to know that the instrument consists of four groups of items; first is a leather airtight bag which acts as an air reservoir and is covered with cloth of a distinctive Regimental colour or tartan; next is a blowpipe; then there is the chanter which is fingered by the piper; finally there are the three drones, of which one is longer than the others and acts as a staff for the pipebanner, if carried. The drones are attached to each other by a tasselled cord or by a length of tartan ribbon.

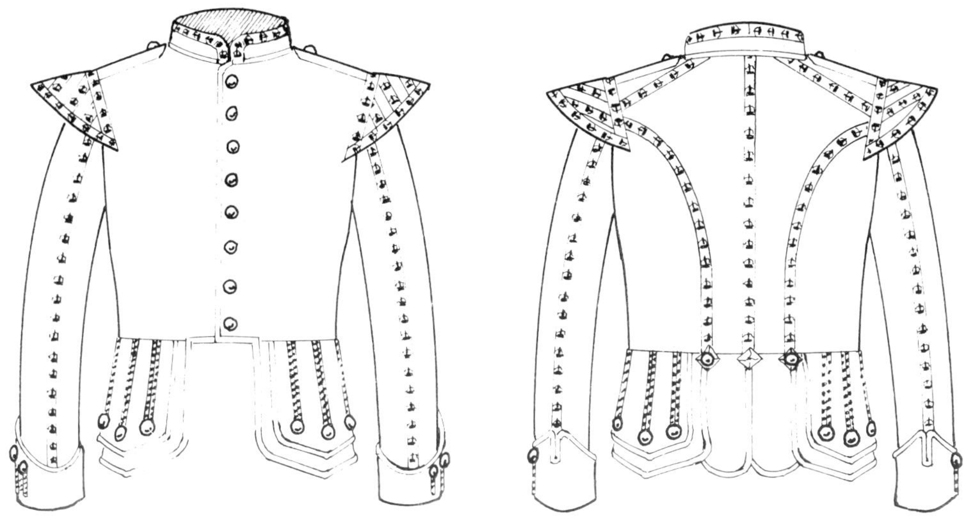

77 Highland Regiment Drummer's Doublet

Other Ranks Undress

For ranks below SSgt, the undress headdress was the glengarry with Regimental diced band, where appropriate, and metal Regimental badge. WOs and SSgts wore either the glengarry (usual in Highland Regiments) or the round peaked cap with diced band and embroidered badge (usual in Lowland Regiments). The undress jacket for WOs of Highland Regiments seems to have been an officer's pattern scarlet shell jacket; this equated to the white serge shell jacket (see **Fig 17**) worn by Sgts (including CSgts) and below. As in the Foot Guards, this garment was perfectly plain save for scarlet worsted badges of rank worn on the right arm. The men of Lowland Regiments, by contrast, all wore a Scottish pattern of frock. This was (see **Fig 80**) scarlet with the collar only in the facing colour, white piping at the base of the collar and around the top and rear of the cuffs, and white lace button holes on the cuffs and pocket-flaps. The practice with regard to collar badges, badges of rank and appointment, and the wearing of valise and other equipment were generally as described elsewhere. Pipers wore a Scottish frock of green material which, like the doublet, showed no facings.

Officers' Full Dress

The full dress headdress for a Regimental officer was the same as that of his men though in the case of the Highland bonnet the tails seemed longer and the hackle larger. The doublet too was cut in the same style as for other ranks and made of scarlet cloth for all except Scottish Rifles. The collar and cuffs were made of the Regimental facing colour and the collar, which was edged with white, was laced by rank as for line infantry (see page 48). The gauntlet cuffs were edged on the top and down the back seam with $\frac{1}{2}$ inch gold lace. The Inverness skirts and pocket flaps were edged with white cloth. On the cuffs and pocket flaps, the buttonholes were of gold russia braid. Shoulder cords and badges of rank were as for Line Infantry. Officers above the rank of Lt had additional lace as follows (see **Fig 74**):

Capt. A line of gold russia braid $\frac{1}{4}$ inch inside the gold lace on the top and rear of the cuffs.

Maj. As for Lt but with a second bar of $\frac{1}{2}$-inch gold lace along the top of the cuffs; in addition, $\frac{1}{2}$-inch gold lace around the skirts and flaps.

Lt Col. As for Maj but with a line of gold russia braid $\frac{1}{4}$ inch inside the gold lace on the top and rear of the cuffs.

Kilts were of regimental pattern, as were sporrans, plaid brooches, dirks and belts, shoulder belt plates, and skean dhu. The shoulder belt worn by the officers and WOs of most Regiments was of white buff leather 3 inches wide; it had two slings hanging from gilt rings (as illustrated in **Fig 84**) and was used by those on dismounted duty for carrying the claymore. Field and other officers when mounted were supposed instead to wear a white leather waistbelt $1\frac{1}{2}$ inches wide with the claymore suspended, as in the remainder of the Infantry, on 1 inch wide slings; practice varied, however. The Highland pattern sash worn by most Regiments was of crimson silk and 15 inches wide in the centre reducing to 7 inches at each end where it was joined together and finished with a fringe; this is why in photographs it never appears quite flat like a Line Infantry officer's sash.

78 *Buglers Highland Light Infantry circa 1896 (Left man in drummer's doublet, right in R&F doublet)*

Officers' Undress

Headdress

There were only two undress items of headdress and Regiments generally wore one or the other. The glengarry was as described elsewhere for the men but with an officer's pattern of metal badge. The round peaked forage cap as described on page 47 was worn by some Regiments with a diced band and a metal or embroidered badge.

Jackets

Generally three were in use. Just as elsewhere in the Line, the dark blue frogged patrol jacket (see page 50) was still common. In some Regiments, the old scarlet shell jacket was also worn; this was a plain short garment piped white all round, with collar and pointed cuffs in the Regimental facing colour and gold shoulder cords bearing badges of rank as in full dress. This jacket should not be confused with the mess jacket which sprang from the same parent but which was required to be edged all round with gold braid (see Dress Regulations 1883 and 1891); eventually it lost its gold braid, at least for Scottish infantry, and the two jackets became one again, described in Dress Regulations 1900 as a "Drill and Mess Jacket". Here of course is an instance, beloved of the Army, of the appropriate orders not so much laying down the way ahead as regularising past practice! The third jacket which is known to have been worn at this time by officers of the Royal Scots Fusiliers, by Mounted Infantry officers of the Royal Scots in Zululand, and possibly by others, was the scarlet serge frock. This was much the same as that of the men (see **Fig 80**) described elsewhere.

The Royal Scots (Lothian Regiment)

Titles:

1633–1637	Le Regiment d'Hebron (Hepburn)
1637–1675	Le Regiment de Douglas
1675–1684	The Earl of Dumbarton's Regiment of Foot
1684–1751	The Royal Regiment of Foot
1751–1812	The 1st or The Royal Regiment of Foot
1812–1821	The 1st Regiment of Foot or Royal Scots
1821–1871	The 1st or The Royal Regiment of Foot
1871–1881	The 1st (The Royal Scots) Regiment
1881–1882	The Lothian Regiment (Royal Scots)
1882–1920	The Royal Scots (The Lothian Regiment)
1920–	The Royal Scots (The Royal Regiment)

Badges:

The Royal Cypher within the Collar of St Andrew with Crown over. Authorised in the Clothing Warrant of 14 Sep 1743.

The White Horse of Hanover and "Nec Aspera Terrent". Authorised in the Clothing Warrant of 14 Sep 1743.

The Sphinx superscribed "Egypt". Authorised 6 Jul 1802.

The Star of The Order of the Thistle.

79 *2nd Lieutenant 2nd Bn Royal Scots circa 1890 (Army Museums Ogilby Trust)*

Battle Honours:

EGYPT AND THE SPINX	6 Jul 1802	MAHEIDPOOR	26 Feb 1823
CORUNNA	20 Feb 1812	AVA	6 Dec 1825
PENINSULA	29 Mar 1815	ALMA	16 Oct 1855
NIAGARA	19 May 1815	INKERMAN	16 Oct 1855
WATERLOO	23 Nov 1815	SEVASTOPOL	16 Oct 1855
BUSACO	21 Jun 1817	TAKU FORTS	4 Nov 1861
ST SEBASTIAN	21 Jun 1817	PEKIN*	4 Nov 1861
SALAMANCA	21 Jun 1817	BLENHEIM	13 Mar 1882
VITTORIA	21 Jun 1817	RAMILLIES	13 Mar 1882
NIVE	21 Jun 1817	OUDENARDE	13 Mar 1882
ST LUCIA	25 Jul 1821	MALPLAQUET	13 Mar 1882
EGMONT-OP-ZEE	25 Jul 1821	LOUISBURG	13 Mar 1882
NAGPORE	26 Feb 1823	*Note: "1860" was added to this Honour on 5 Jun 1914.	

Establishments, Strengths and Locations:

		Offrs	WOs	Sgts	Dmrs	R&F	Total
1st Bn	**Establishment**	28	2	46	16	800	892
	Strength	29	2	42	13	597	683
	Location	Natal (arrived South Africa Nov 1884)					
2nd Bn	**Establishment**	24	2	47	16	920	1009
	Strength	24	2	47	16	905	994
	Location	Aldershot (arrived Apr 1888)					
Depot		Glencorse					

Uniform

There are eleven drawings in the original series for the Army and Navy Gazette showing Scottish infantry and only three make any attempt to get away from a standard composition of officer, soldier and piper such as we have here. However, if the group is unimaginative the details and the story are not. For instance, the Royal Scots claim the longest continuous existence of all, beginning in the service of the King of France, and were more recently the 1st Foot on the British establishment. In 1983 they celebrated their 350th birthday and even possibly their nickname of "Pontius Pilate's Bodyguard". This is said to have sprung from an early wrangle with the French Picardy Regiment about their respective antiquity. Picardy claimed to have been on duty as long ago as the night of the Cruxifixion. The Royal Scots are reputed to have capped this with the remark "Had we have been on duty, we would not have slept at our posts!"

It seems likely that Simkin based his drawing on the dress of the 2nd Bn at Aldershot in the late 1880s or early 1890. They were one of the battalions who were issued with the experimental white helmet (see page 50) worn by the bugler in **Fig 82**. Simkin's officer is drawn correctly for the period. The basic helmet plate *(10)* featured magnificently the Star of the Order of the Thistle in gilt with, in the centre, a silver thistle within a silver circlet pierced with the motto "Nemo Me Impune Lacessit" all on a green enamel ground; below was a silver scroll "The Royal Scots". The doublet was as shown elsewhere with a thistle badge embroidered in gold on the collar. The white sword belt was as described above with an oblong gilt plate clasp; this featured as on the helmet plate the star, cross and thistle device of the Order in silver and the circlet and motto in gilt on a green enamel ground. (This is contrary to both 1883 and 1891 Dress Regulations.) The trews worn by officers and soldiers alike in the Royal Scots were similar to the Black Watch or Government sett and known as the "McChilders". This was a reference to the unpopular Secretary of State for War who was responsible for pushing through the 1881 Army organisational reforms. The boots and leggings were as for Line Infantry. (**Fig 79** shows what a 2Lt looked like in undress. His dark blue forage cap had a red, white and blue diced band and a cap badge of the Order of the Thistle exactly the same as for officers of the Scots Guards; the black peak was edged with a broad band of gold embroidery. The trews were Regimental tartan and his claymore, suspended from the white sword belt worn under the jacket, was fitted with the undress cross-bar hilt.) Readers should note that besides the

doublet, tartan trews and claymore, the Highland sash was the only Scottish item to be worn by officers of this Regiment.

The Private wears the same headdress as his officers with similar yellow metal fittings and a yellow metal universal helmet plate *(10)* incorporating a large white metal star in the centre with, over it, a yellow metal St Andrew and Cross. The latter was backed with red cloth by the 1st Bn and with green by the 2nd. His Scottish pattern frock is correctly shown (see the CSgt on the left of **Fig 80**) with white piping or braid on the base of the collar, on the cuffs and in lines on the two pockets only (note that these are not Inverness flaps). The blue collar has brass collar badges of a thistle between two leaves upon a scroll "ROYAL SCOTS". The scarlet shoulder straps were embroidered "RS" in white. Other items of dress and personal equipment are as described elsewhere, including the spare magazine pouch (see page 22) and the intrenching implement behind the left arm.

The piper was a comparatively new figure in the Regiment having been introduced in 1881. His uniform was as for other

80 *Sergeant Major (centre) and Sergeants, 2nd Bn Royal Scots circa 1890 (Army Museums Ogilby Trust)*

Scottish Regiments with a blue glengarry, green doublet and other items and embellishments of Regimental pattern. In the event, pipers of the 1st Bn ended up wearing kilt and plaid of the Regimental tartan while those of the 2nd Bn (see **Fig 81**) wore the Royal Stewart (until 1892 when they left for India and also adopted the Regimental tartan because, it is said, it faded less quickly in the sun). The hose should have been as for the Black Watch (who wore diced red and black) but the 2nd Bn seem to have adopted not the Royal stewart shown by Simkin but the Hunting Stewart (see **Fig 81**); it is of interest that the Regiment tried for some time to obtain permission to convert all items of dress to this sett and succeeded only in 1901. The garter flashes were green and the spats had white buttons. Reverting now to the head, the blue glengarry was embellished with a red toorie, and black rosette on which was fixed the Regimental badge in yellow and white metal (as in the centre of the helmet plate) with above it the distinctive blackcock's feathers. The doublet was all green and piped in white on the base of the collar, around the wings, on the cuffs and on the Inverness skirts. The collar badges and buttons were as for rank and file. The plaid brooch and waistbelt clasp were both white metal, featuring the badge of St Andrew and Cross. The buckle, slide and tip on the baldrick were plain white metal, all

82 *Drummers 2nd Bn Royal Scots circa 1890 (Army Museums Ogilby Trust)*

belts of course being black leather. The dirk was essentially black in colour, its scabbard embellished chiefly in white metal to a Regimental design. The sporran was attached with a black leather strap and had a black cantle edged with white metal and bearing a white metal badge of St Andrew and Cross within a wreath; on white goat's hair there were two black tassels with white metal caps. The pipes seem to have had a bag of the Regimental tartan and the drones to be tied with a green cord and tassels as well as (in the 2nd Bn) with a length of Royal Stewart tartan ribbon. Pipers' uniforms are a minefield for the unwary and the author is left with at least one small mystery: the wings on the doublet drawn by Simkin are double layered which does not agree with the author's knowledge of either 1st or 2nd Bn at this time.

Finally, **Fig 82** is included for interest because it shows Drummers in both full and undress. Points to note in the former are the crown and inch lace on the top of the collar, the wings, the sleeves and (as in **Fig 78**) on the back of the doublet; no drum badge on the right sleeve; plain brass drum shell and universal hoops, painted blue, edged red and with a white worm through the middle. In the case of the man in undress, the piping on his frock is in red/white worsted material, and he has a drum badge on the right arm; his bugle cord is red, blue and yellow (for a Royal Regiment) and he wears a drummer's sword. Other items in both cases are as for rank and file.

81 *Piper 2nd Bn Royal Scots circa 1890 (Army Museums Ogilby Trust)*

The Gordon Highlanders

Titles:

1st Battalion

1787–1809	The 75th (Highland) Regiment of Foot
1809–1862	The 75th Regiment of Foot
1862–1881	The 75th (Stirlingshire) Regiment of Foot

2nd Battalion

1794–1799	The 100th (Gordon Highland) Regiment of Foot. Renumbered.
1799–1861	The 92nd (Highland) Regiment of Foot
1861–1881	The 92nd (Gordon Highlanders) Regiment of Foot
1881–	The Gordon Highlanders

Badges:

The Royal Tiger. Authorised to the 75th, 6 Jul 1807.

The Sphinx superscribed "Egypt". Authorised to the 92nd, 6 Jul 1802.

The Head of a Stag (the crest of the Marquis of Huntley who raised the 92nd) issuing from a ducal coronet and with a wreath of ivy (the badge of the Gordon family).

The Motto: "Bydand" (Watchful).

The Star of the Order of the Thistle.

Battle Honours:

(2)	EGYPT AND THE SPHINX	6 Jul 1802
(1)	INDIA WITH THE ROYAL TIGER	6 Jul 1807
(2)	BERGEN-OP-ZEE	15 Feb 1813
	Changed to EGMONT-OP-ZEE	31 Aug 1814
(2)	MANDORA	15 Feb 1813
(2)	PENINSULA	6 Apr 1815
(2)	WATERLOO	8 Dec 1815
(1)	SERINGAPATAM	28 May 1818
(2)	CORUNNA	16 Feb 1830
(2)	FUENTES D'ONOR	16 Feb 1830
(2)	ALMARAZ	16 Feb 1830
(2)	VITTORIA	16 Feb 1830
(2)	PYRENEES	16 Feb 1830
(2)	NIVE	16 Feb 1830
(2)	ORTHES	16 Feb 1830
(1)	MYSORE	12 Feb 1889
(1)	SOUTH AFRICA 1835	25 Jul 1882
(1)	DELHI 1857	3 Sep 1863
(1)	LUCKNOW	3 Sep 1863
(2)	CHARASIAH	GO 56/1881
(2)	KABUL, 1879	GO 56/1881
(2)	KANDAHAR, 1880	GO 56/1881
(2)	AFGHANISTAN, 1878–80	GO 56/1881
	EGYPT 1882, 1884	GO 32/1883
	("1884" added GO 10/1885)	
	TEL-EL-KEBIR	GO 32/1883
	NILE, 1884–85	GO 10/1886

Establishments, Strengths and Locations:

		Offrs	WOs	Sgts	Dmrs	R&F	Total
1st Bn	Establishment	28	2	47	21	800	898
	Strength	27	2	38	20	745	832
	Location	Ceylon (arrived Dec 1888)					
2nd Bn	Establishment	24	2	40	21	720	807
	Strength	24	2	38	21	581	666
	Location	Belfast (arrived Aug 1887)					
Depot		Aberdeen					

Uniform

Simkin's drawing is dated 1891 and seems to be based on the dress of the Regiment over the previous six years or so. In the author's opinion, the Piper for example, was drawn from the photo at **Fig 87**, though there are two particular differences as we shall see below. The Piper in the photograph, and also Simkin's CSgt, hold the medal for the 2nd Afghan War in which the 2nd Bn had taken part.

The officer seems to be generally correct though the details are sometimes awry. He may be compared with the officer seated in the centre of **Fig 83** and with **Fig 84**. From the latter it will be seen that the (red, white and green) diced band on the bonnet was effectively covered by the ostrich feathers. Though they cannot be counted in any of the illustrations, five tails should have fallen to the wearer's right shoulder (and no doubt did !). On the other side of the bonnet, the large silver stag's head badge, one of the most famous in the Army, was set on a black silk cocade. The doublet with its chrome yellow facings is in accordance with the regulations as are the kilt and plaid in the Gordon tartan; this was the Government sett with an additional yellow line adopted by the 92nd on formation and taken over by the 75th on amalgamation in 1881. The plaid brooch is perhaps a little high in Simkin's drawing, and the antlers are definitely more aggressively proud than they should be but the general effect compares not unfavourably with contemporary photographs. The (waist or) dirk belt was made of leather embellished with three lines of gold thistle pattern lace with, in the case of the Gordons, a black line at top and bottom. (The same lace of course embellished the doublet.)

The clasp was a gilt plate with the badge superimposed in silver; this consisted of the Sphinx and "EGYPT" over the tiger and "INDIA" within a circlet consisting of a label "GORDON HIGHLANDERS" at the top and a thistle wreath below all on a cross of St Andrew. The dirk and scabbard were black with silver fittings featuring acanthus leaf work at the hilt, a regimental badge (as on the waistbelt plate) on the upper mounting on the scabbard, and thistle design on the other mountings. This weapon, or the officer's gloves, serve to hide a white metal kilt pin in Simkin's drawing. The shoulder belt plate was gilt with silvered design of a star, cross and badges superimposed (see *(23)* p757 and *(25)* p196 for a drawing wrongly described in each case as the device on "waist-plates and buttons"). The dress sporran is indicated correctly as white hair with five gold bullion tassels; the cantle was gilt, engraved with thistle designs, and set at the top with the same badge in silver as on the waistbelt clasp. The claymore carried by a company officer, with a full basket hilt, contrasts with the sword carried by field officers (see **Fig 84**) with a half-basket. All ranks of the Gordons wore red and black hose tops with scarlet garter flashes arranged as a pair with a loop or tuck in them, as can be seen in **Figs 83** and **85**. Simkin has correctly shown them and the spats, the latter with the distinctive black buttons worn by all ranks. (It is amusing to note from the Clothing Department records that these were bone buttons of the same pattern as those used to secure Gentlemen Cadets' trousers !).

The dress of the R&F is shown at **Fig 85**. It is not known for

83 *Veterans of Egypt campaign, 1st Bn Gordon Highlanders, Ceylon circa 1891. (Left to right, standing: Corporal, Sergeant Major, Lieutenant (possibly the Quartermaster), Band Sergeant, Sergeant.)*

84 *Lieutenant Colonel G S White VC, CB, Gordon Highlanders circa 1885*

85 *Guard of 2nd Bn Gordon Highlanders circa 1894 (Army Museums Ogilby Trust)*

certain how many tails the bonnet actually had but the author is convinced it was four. In other respects it was generally like the officer's except that the cocade was of black leather. The doublet was faced with yellow and piped with white; the scarlet shoulder straps were embroidered at the end in white with "GORDON" in a slight curve; the collar badges were brass tigers facing inwards; the kilt was generally like the officer's, including the pin. At this time, both the 1st and 2nd Bns were still wearing the 1882 valise equipment and waistbelt though they had received the Lee-Metford; this situation is illustrated by Simkin. The rank and file sporran was of white hair with two black hair tassels depending from brass caps; the cantle was black leather with a broad brass upper edging and a small brass shield set centrally showing the stag's head over a coronet with the motto "BYDAND" above. The hose tops, garter flashes and spats were as for the officer.

A CSgt (see **Fig 86**) wore a better quality doublet but was otherwise dressed much the same except for four important differences: his badge of rank was as for Infantry (crown over crossed Union Flags over three gold lace chevrons on scarlet); he wore a fly plaid in review order secured with a round silvered brooch set with the badge worn by officers on the waistbelt clasp (see description above); thirdly (and contrary to Simkin) his sporran cantle was brass and set with the same silvered badge (to look like a plainer version of the officer's sporran); lastly he wore of course a Sgt's sash. WOs and SSgts, however, were a different matter and edged much more closely towards the officer's dress. See **Fig 83** and note for example: gold-laced collar but the absence of collar badges; officer's sash worn by the Sergeant Major; Sergeant's sash worn over

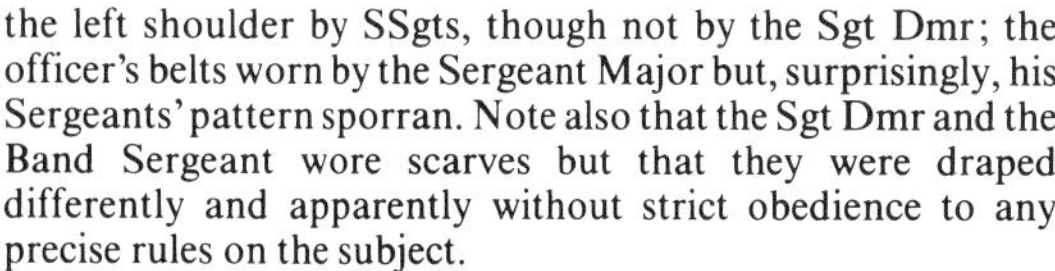

86 *Colour Sergeants Gordon Highlanders circa 1891*

87 *Piper 2nd Bn Gordon Highlanders circa 1884 (Army Museums Ogilby Trust)*

the left shoulder by SSgts, though not by the Sgt Dmr; the officer's belts worn by the Sergeant Major but, surprisingly, his Sergeants' pattern sporran. Note also that the Sgt Dmr and the Band Sergeant wore scarves but that they were draped differently and apparently without strict obedience to any precise rules on the subject.

Pipers wore a plain blue glengarry with a red tuft and black silk band and tails; the cocade was of black silk and the badge as for all ranks; the feather was a blackcock's. The doublet was all green with white piping at the base of the collar, down the chest, on and around the wings (but not the shoulder straps) and the cuffs, and on the skirts as shown in **Fig 87**. The buttons and tiger collar badges were brass as for rank and file. (At this point it should be noted that **Fig 87** and Simkin's Piper are of the 2nd Bn; those of the 1st Bn wore rather different wings,

sporran cantles and belt clasps and embellishments which are not illustrated in this book nor described any further.) The black (waist or) dirk belt was fastened with a large oblong silvered clasp just visible in **Fig 87**; it had an oval hole in the centre and was embossed with a thistle design. A very similar plate acted as baldrick buckle up towards his right shoulder; lower down the slide and tip were of similar design (and are quite well illustrated in another photo of the same man in "Uniform of the Scottish Infantry 1740–1900" published in paperback by HMSO in 1970, which may still be available); in the 1880s there was no other badge on the baldrick. However, by 1890, a new and more conventionally shaped buckle had been introduced together with a silvered badge above it; this was the St Andrew's Cross with label, wreath, Sphinx and tiger as on the officers' waistbelt clasp and the Pipers' plaid brooch.

It is not known whether the new buckle and the badge arrived simultaneously but it is interesting that Simkin has the badge only. He has also shown correctly the silvered sporran cantle adopted by 1890 in place of the brass mounted ORs pattern worn by the piper in **Fig 87**. The kilt and scarf were of the Regimental sett, and it seems likely that the scarf was worn over the baldrick at this time. The design of the dirk is not clear but it was probably much like that of an officer. The plaid brooch cannot be seen at all but was the same as, or very similar to, that of a Sergeant. Finally, the pipes are shown quite well in **Fig 87**, the drones held together with green cord and the bag encased in Regimental tartan. Simkin has correctly shown the drones secured in addition with tartan ribbon.

The Queen's Own Cameron Highlanders

Titles:

1793–1804	The 79th (Cameronian Volunteers) Regiment of Foot
1804–1873	The 79th (Cameron Highlanders) Regiment of Foot
1873–1881	The 79th (Queen's Own Cameron Highlanders) Regiment
1881–1961	The Queen's Own Cameron Highlanders

Amalgamation with The Seaforth Highlanders (Ross-shire Buffs, The Duke of Albany's)

1961–	The Queen's Own Highlanders (Seaforth and Camerons)

Badges:

The Sphinx superscribed "Egypt". Authorised 6 Jul 1802.

The Thistle ensigned with the Imperial Crown. Authorised with the change of title, 12 May 1873.

Battle Honours:

EGYPT AND THE SPHINX	6 Jul 1802
PENINSULA	6 Apr 1815
WATERLOO	8 Dec 1815
TOULOUSE	9 Jul 1816
FUENTES D'ONOR	16 Apr 1818
SALAMANCA	16 Apr 1818
PYRENEES	16 Apr 1818
NIVELLE	16 Apr 1818
NIVE	16 Apr 1818
EGMONT-OP-ZEE	2 Oct 1818
ALMA	16 Oct 1855
SEVASTOPOL	16 Oct 1855
LUCKNOW	3 Sep 1863
EGYPT, 1882	GO 32/1883
TEL-EL-KEBIR	GO 32/1883
NILE, 1884–85	GO 10/1886

88 *Types of Cameron Highlanders circa 1890 (Army Museums Ogilby Trust)*

Establishments, Strengths and Locations:

	Offrs	WOs	Sgts	Dmrs	R&F	Total
Establishment	24	2	40	21	720	807
Strength	24	2	39	21	675	761
Location	Edinburgh (arrived Mar 1888)					
Depot	Inverness					

Uniform

The Queen's Own Cameron Highlanders were unique among the infantry of 1890 in that they had only one regular battalion. In 1887 even this had come under fire with a determined attempt to convert it into a 3rd Bn of the Scots Guards. Not long before, the whole Highland Infantry had survived an attempt to exchange the feather bonnet for a helmet adorned with the lion of Scotland. In both cases, victory was obtained with the help of a public outcry which was probably without equal until the successful Mitchell campaign to save the Argylls some eighty years later. One suspects that people in

89 *Cameron Highlanders circa 1887 (Army Museums Ogilby Trust)*

90 *Colour Sergeant McNeil, Cameron Highlanders circa 1890 (Army Museums Ogilby Trust)*

1890 were quite well informed on the Camerons and their Scots dress!

Simkin's private soldier is broadly correct. His bonnet almost certainly had four tails although the Regimental custom of the 79th was for five. The diced band was red, white and green but at this time was almost totally obscured by the ostrich feathers. The white metal badge consisted of St Andrew with the Cross surrounded by a wreath of thistles. The scarlet tunic had blue facings on the collar and cuffs, and very much smaller collar badges in white metal (see **Fig 88**) than Simkin shows. The scarlet shoulder straps were embroidered at the ends with "CAMERON" in white on a curve (see **Fig 89**). The kilt was made of Cameron of Erracht tartan, which was unique to the Regiment. The sporran was of black hair with two white tassels; the cantle was of black leather embellished with a white metal badge of the same design as that worn on the bonnet; the strap was black. The hose tops were green and red (badly shown by Simkin) worn with red garter flashes and white spats with white buttons. Simkin's drawing has two other interesting

92 Officer Cameron Highlanders (Levee Order) circa 1895 (Army Museums Ogilby Trust)

91 Colour Sergeant, Cameron Highlanders circa 1892

points; the first is that like the men in **Fig 89**, his Private wears an 1882 pattern waistbelt; unlike them he carries a Lee-Metford rifle. The date on which this was issued in place of the Martini-Henry is not known but it was probably early 1892; "before" and "after" are well illustrated by the CSgt in **Figs 90** and **91**. Valise equipment pattern 1888 was evidently later still. The second point is that Simkin's Private seems to be wearing (see below his left hand) a belted fly. This is confirmed by the centre and right hand man in **Fig 89**. However this item of dress was not officially issued to them. It was probably provided on a Regimental basis at their own expense though whether it was worn on all occasions is not clear.

The officer, unlike his men, had a bonnet with five tails though other details were similar. The doublet was faced blue and laced with gold (thistle design) as shown in **Fig 92**. Simkin has shown this adequately together with the large silver embroidered collar badges. However, he did not do so well with the dirk and belt; the latter was of blue leather embroidered with a design of thistles in silver and their leaves in gold, with a round gilt clasp featuring the Regimental badge in silver. The hilt and scabbard of the dirk were black with gilt mountings. The dress sporran was of grey goat's hair with a black strap, and Simkin has shown this fairly well except that he has skimped on the detail of the gilt cantle with its small silver crowned thistle and the tassels which are of gold bullion suspended from twisted gold and blue cords. The plaid brooch was silver and consisted of the Sphinx over "EGYPT" with "PENINSULA" above and "WATERLOO" below, all surrounded by a wreath of thistles. (All these articles are excellently illustrated in the catalogue for Wallis & Wallis Autumn 1984 Sale, lot 34.)

The shoulder belt plate is not clear from any of the illustrations; it was rectangular gilt with a silver cross of St

94 Pipe Banner Cameron Highlanders late nineteenth century

Andrew, with upon that, a silver crowned thistle within an oval gilt crowned collar; below the cross was a silver Sphinx over "EGYPT". As a final note on the officer, it should be seen that Simkin has correctly shown him in a belted plaid; by contrast, the subject of **Fig 92** is in levee dress and, equally correctly for the Camerons, wears a scarf.

Simkin's Piper is not his most accurate work and although the main features are alright several of the details are poorly or quite inaccurately shown. He wears correctly a blue glengarry with a white metal R&F badge and a single feather; this was actually from a golden eagle and therefore should be gold to brown in colour, but not black! The green doublet was piped with white, including all round the shoulder strap, (though not on the seams of the sleeves and back) and set with white metal diamond-shape buttons. The collar badges were as for R&F and smaller than those shown by the artist. He has also shown the wrong waistbelt clasp which should have been like the officer's (see **Fig 93**). The sporran is broadly, if rather crudely, correct with the studded white metal edge to the cantle and the same badge as for R&F. However, the plaid brooch is quite wrong and should be a plain circle for a Piper as opposed to the more ornate version worn by the Sergeant Piper (see these contrasted in **Fig 88**). Simkin has shown the hose in the right colours but they are poorly drawn; great care was always taken in Highland Regiments to make sure that the diced design matched all the way down from the cuff. The pipes were secured with a green tasselled cord, and also with a tartan ribbon which was pinned on over the cord. 1st Bn Pipers carried a blue banner (see **Fig 94**) with a small union in the upper canton, a gold fringe and blue ribbons securing it to the drone; both sides were the same and featured a device of a crown in full colours over a thistle (white over purple with green leaves) over "LXXIX" in gold all within a wreath of green oakleaves with brown acorns, tied with a red and white ribbon; below this was a Sphinx in white, facing towards the drone. The Sergeant Piper's banner was more ornate.

93 Pipers Cameron Highlanders circa 1887 (Army Museums Ogilby Trust)

THE RIFLES

General Introduction

In 1890 there were four Regiments of Rifles. The Scottish and the Irish were both formed in 1881 on the reorganisation of the Line, and were both removed from the Army List in 1968. The King's Royal Rifles and the Rifle Brigade, however, were formed much earlier and continue as Greenjackets to this day; it is with the former that this section is mostly concerned though it can be applied in general terms to the Rifle Brigade and the Royal Irish Rifles as well. Nonetheless the reader is encouraged not to make assumptions, and certainly not in relation to the Scottish Rifles whose dress was unique.

Riflemen, even today, have a number of peculiarities, some of which they share with the new (i.e. 1968 formation) Light Infantry. Besides rifle (or very dark, verging on black) green uniforms, they wear black buttons on practically every article of clothing; they march on parade at 140 paces to the minute – which is actually quite fast and worth looking out for; they have no Colours nor a Corps of Drums; they do not fix bayonets on ceremonial parades and in any case call them "swords", a custom dating back to the issue of the first rifle in 1794 which would not take a bayonet and was therefore accompanied by a sword; they have no position of attention on parade but begin and end drill movements from the "At Ease"; last, and certainly not least, they are immensely successful at getting their officers to the upper echelons of the Army. These idiosyncracies have earned for them the rather unkind nickname of the "Black Mafia".

This section now looks in general terms at the uniform of the Rifles.

Full Dress Headdress

1890 was a year of change because in the summer it was approved that Rifles could discontinue use of the unpopular home service helmet and resume the busby, though of a new folding design. Both headdresses might therefore have been seen though probably not together in the same battalion.

The Home Service Helmet: This was covered with dark green material and was as described on page 44 (being the same basic helmet as issued to Light Infantry) except that the fittings were of bronze (i.e. virtually blackened) metal.

The Busby: The other ranks' version was made of black sealskin 5 inches high rising to 6 inches high in the centre and it had a rifle green top. On the front, at the top, was a black corded boss with a Regimental device on it. The busby was ornamented with double black cords, the length in front plaited and sewn down. There was also a black patent leather chin strap. The officers' version was of astrakhan wool (actually black Persian lambskin) with a rifle green cloth top, and black cord embellishments which consisted of: an oval cord boss on the front with a small Regimental device on it; a double length of black cord around the cap which was plaited round the front, embellished at the centre of the top of each side with a small bronze bugle badge, and secured with a ring at the rear; black body lines were attached here, as for an Hussar, with a swivel clip; black patent leather chin strap; below the boss, a Regimental badge; above the boss, from a bronze ball socket with upright leaves, a $6\frac{1}{2}$-inch plume of Regimental pattern.

Other Ranks' Full Dress

The full dress tunic for rank and file was cut much as for Line Infantry but was made of course of rifle green cloth. The principal difference lay in the cuffs which were green and pointed; collar badges were not worn. The trousers were also rifle green and without a stripe or welt.

Distinction of Rank: As with other groups, tunics of better quality but without any special lace were provided for Sgts and SSgts. WOs were provided probably under Regimental arrangements with tunics of officer's pattern. Badges of rank, and of appointment where it was aligned to rank, were generally as for other groups except they were made of mostly black material. There were Regimental variations of colouring and for lack of space no exhaustive list is given here. The CSgt's badge was, however, quite different: above three chevrons, there was a device of a crown above crossed swords above two stringed bugles intertwined. Until 1887 this had been ordered to be surrounded by a wreath and examples of this version (6) may still have been in wear in 1890.

Proficiency Badges: As for rank and appointment, most badges of proficiency (see (24) for a definition and details) were the same as for other infantry though they varied in colour by Regiments for ranks below Sgt; above that rank badges were the universal pattern in gold and colours. Several badges were, however, different including a pioneer's (crossed axes surmounted by a stringed bugle) and a Bugler's (two stringed bugles intertwined, worn on the frock only).

Personal Equipment: The valise equipment issued to Rifles was black, including the haversack. Its design and use was otherwise the same as for other Infantry with the following exceptions: the waistbelt was fastened with a yellow metal snake hook; the rifle sling was attached to the butt or lower sling swivel and left slack (see **Fig 95**); thirdly, the sword belt and slings for WOs and SSgts was of black leather and was worn, like the officer's, under the tunic.

Buglers: A Bugler's tunic was specially laced according to Regiment. There were no drummers except in the Band.

95 *Sergeant King's Royal Rifle Corps circa 1891*

Other Ranks' Undress

Headdress: The standard undress headdress for Sgts (including CSgts) and below was a green glengarry as described on page 47 for Light Infantry. WOs and SSgts wore a dark green pill-box, or peakless version of the cap described on page 47 for Light Infantry. As in other groups, this was the officers' undress cap; it was worn towards the right side of the head and was kept on with a black patent leather strap.

Jacket: Sgts (including CSgts) and R&F wore a black, five-button, frock with pockets and flaps in the front skirts. This had Regimental embellishments which are described below for KRRC. SSgts wore a special pattern of button-less frock edged all round with inch black braid; the author is not clear how this was embellished Regimentally and therefore no further details are given in this book. WOs (and possibly also the Regimental Quartermaster Sergeant) wore an officer's pattern patrol jacket as described below.

Other Garments: Trousers, boots and leggings, when ordered, were as for full dress.

Officers' Full Dress

The tunic (see **Fig 97**) was rifle green with the collar and cuffs in the facing colour; like many other articles of an officer's dress it was in the style affected by Hussars, having black cord edging all round except the collar, black cord loops down the chest (though 5 instead of the Hussar's 6), black cord on the seams of the back, and a system of braid and cord on the collar and cuffs denoting rank. The trousers were rifle-green with a 2 inch wide black braid stripe. In place of a Line officer's sash, Rifle officers wore a black patent leather cross belt 3 inches wide with a black patent leather pouch on the back, and a silver or silvered Regimental badge and other fittings. The sword belt was worn under the tunic and supported black patent leather sword slings 1 inch wide and, for mounted officers, black patent leather sabretache slings ¾ inch wide; the sword was as described on page 19 and worn with a black leather strap and acorn; the sabretache was black patent leather with a silver stringed bugle badge 2¾ inches high.

96 *General Sir R H Buller VC circa 1897, as Colonel King's Royal Rifle Corps*

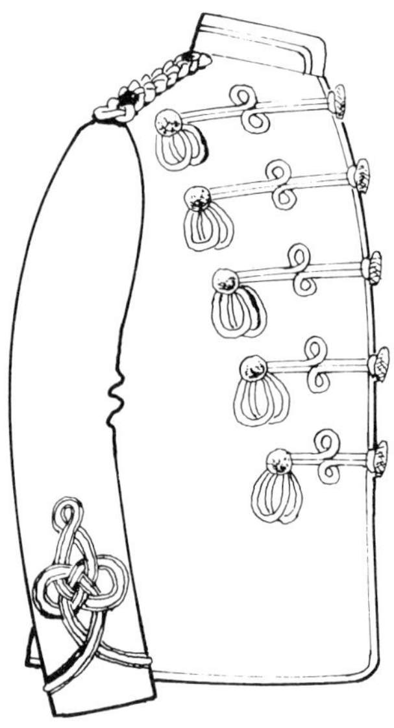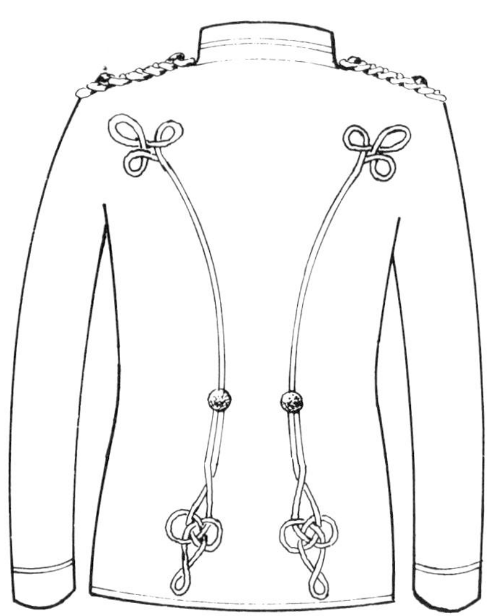

97 *Tunic, Lieutenant King's Royal Rifle Corps*

Officers' Undress

The round green pill-box cap has been described above and is illustrated in **Fig 99**. Two jackets were in use, a frogged patrol jacket and a plain frock. Both were ordered to be dark green but were of Regimental pattern; the patrol jacket appropriate to KRRC is described below. The frock, despite the regulations, was probably made of black rather than green serge. Although this would have matched the men's frocks, it has to be said that evidence is rather thin and anyway that there was almost no difference between the two colours! This area requires further research.

The King's Royal Rifle Corps

Titles:

1755–1757	The 62nd (Royal American) Regiment of Foot
1757–1815	The 60th (Royal American) Regiment of Foot
1815–1824	The 60th (Royal American) Light Infantry
1824 (Jun)	The 60th Royal American Regiment
1824 (Jul)	The 60th (The Duke of York's Own)
1824 (Aug)	The 60th (Duke of York's Own Rifle Corps)
1824 (Sep)–1830	The 60th Duke of York's Own Rifle Corps
1830–1881	The 60th King's Royal Rifle Corps
1881–1920	The King's Royal Rifle Corps
1920–1921	The King's Royal Rifles
1921–1958	The King's Royal Rifle Corps
1958–1966	2nd Green Jackets, The King's Royal Rifle Corps

Absorbed into The Royal Green Jackets

1966–1968	The 2nd Bn, The Royal Green Jackets (The King's Royal Rifle Corps)
1968–	The 2nd Bn, The Royal Green Jackets

Badges:

The Maltese Cross with Crown.
Motto: "Celer et Audax".
A Bugle Horn.

Battle Honours:

PENINSULA	6 Apr 1815	PUNJAUB	14 Dec 1852
MARTINIQUE	28 Aug 1817	MOOLTAN	14 Dec 1852
ROLEIA	21 Sep 1821	GOOJERAT	14 Dec 1852
VIMIERA	21 Sep 1821	TAKU FORTS	4 Nov 1861
TALAVERA	21 Sep 1821	PEKIN	4 Nov 1861
FUENTES D'ONOR	21 Sep 1821	DELHI	3 Sep 1863
CUIDAD RODRIGO	21 Sep 1821	BUSACO	25 Apr 1879
BADAJOZ	21 Sep 1821	AHMAD KHEL	GO 56/1881
SALAMANCA	21 Sep 1821	KANDAHAR 1880	GO 56/1881
VITTORIA	21 Sep 1821	AFGHANISTAN 1878–80	GO 56/1881
NIVELLE	21 Sep 1821	LOUISBURG	13 Mar 1882
ORTHES	21 Sep 1821	QUEBEC 1759	13 Mar 1882
TOULOUSE	21 Sep 1821	SOUTH AFRICA 1851–2–3, 1879	25 Jul 1882
ALBUHERA	12 Jan 1825	EGYPT 1882, 1884	GO 32/1883
PYRENEES	12 Jan 1825		("1884" added: GO 10/1885)
NIVE	12 Jan 1825	TEL-EL-KEBIR	GO 32/1883

Establishments, Strengths and Locations:

1st Bn		Offrs	WOs	Sgts	Dmrs	R&F	Total
	Establishment	24	2	47	16	920	1009
	Strength	22	2	46	16	904	990
	Location	Aldershot (arrived May 1888)					
2nd Bn	**Establishment**	24	2	39	16	720	801
	Strength	24	2	37	15	579	657
	Location	Enniskillen (arrived Jan 1888)					

3rd Bn	**Establishment**	28	2	46	16	800	892
	Strength	27	2	47	16	803	895
	Location	Gibraltar (arrived Jun 1886)					
4th Bn	**Establishment**	28	2	45	16	920	1011
	Strength	26	2	46	16	982	1072
	Location	Chakrata, Bengal (arrived Dec 1876)					
Depot		Winchester					

Uniform

The Army & Navy Gazette print based on Simkin's drawing reproduced in Plate 18 was published in 1895. But the drawing is dated 1891 and seems accurate for that year except for one or two minor details, and a possible argument over the colour of the uniforms. Close examination of the drawing suggests that they are grey indicating black; this is correct for the Bugler and the Rifleman but may be wrong for the officer. Perhaps Simkin made an assumption or maybe a degree of green has faded over the years. By contrast The Army & Navy Gazette colourist was under no illusions and put everyone in rifle green throughout – which was certainly wrong!

Simkin's Private or Rifleman is in skeleton Field Day Order; in other words, he has no equipment but his waistbelt and water bottle. This seems unlikely, as does the way in which he is carrying his rifle; the Gazette passed over the first point but interestingly moved his right arm and rifle down. There is no way of knowing the evidence upon which the state of equipment illustrated was based, but we do know that the 1st Bn received the Lee-Metford rifle in Jan 1890 (only to exchange it back again in Oct the same year for the Martini-Henry prior to moving to India!). The 3rd Bn on the other hand had to wait until Apr 1892 before receiving the Lee-Metford. Concerning valise equipment, the 2nd Bn was issued with pattern 1888 in May 1890 (and with the new busbies in Dec that year); the 1st Bn in Aldershot probably received both a little earlier.

The helmet badge of both officers and ORs was in the form of a bronze crowned Maltese cross (see **Fig 98**) with the centre backed with scarlet. The OR's busby had a black cord boss with a bronze Maltese cross badge on it, and a black out of scarlet plume; the scarlet part was secured with a bronze ring. The officer's busby had a bronze crown on the boss, a bronze Maltese cross below it and a plume of black egret feathers out of short scarlet vulture feathers – points well shown in **Fig 96**.

The OR's tunic had a scarlet collar edged on the front and top with ½-inch black braid; the pointed cuffs were similarly edged with black braid itself edged above with scarlet piping; the front of the tunic which had seven buttons was edged scarlet; two lines of scarlet piping fell to the rear skirts from buttons set at the waist (exactly in the manner of Line Infantry tunics); the shoulder straps were green and were embroidered "KRR" in scarlet in a straight line across the end; all buttons were of black bone. The OR's frock was a plain black garment with scarlet piping around the base of the collar; scarlet piping around the pointed cuffs coming to a single loop above the point; black shoulder straps embroidered with "KRR" in scarlet as on the tunic; black buttons. Badges of rank, appoint-

ment and proficiency were (with effect from a change made in 1889) of black lace or embroidery on scarlet cloth backing; an exception to this may have been the signaller's badge which seems to have been standardised for all Rifle Regiments as black embroidery on green cloth. The same badges were worn on the undress frock except that the complex colour badge was

98 *Officer's Helmet King's Royal Rifle Corps circa 1890 (Army Museums Ogilby Trust)*

reduced, mirroring the Line practise, to a crown over the three chevrons. Careful examination of Simkin's drawing reveals the suggestion of a badge on the Bugler's upper right arm; the author believes it should have been there.

The officer's tunic (**Fig 97**) had scarlet collar and cuffs; the skirts rounded in front and closed behind; five loops of black, square cord on the chest with netted caps and drops (or loops), fastened with black olivets; on each back seam, the same cord forming a trefoil at the top and an austrian knot at the bottom of the skirt; shoulder cords of black chain gimp with black buttons and bronze badges of rank (as on page 48). Lace was as follows:

Collar. 2Lt –Lt: Black ½-inch braid on the front and top of the collar with, inside it, a line of black russia braid. Capt: The same ½-inch black braid with, inside it, a row of braided eyes. Maj – Col: The same ½-inch black braid with, inside it, a row of figured braiding.

Cuffs. 2Lt – Lt: Black cord austrian knot edged throughout with tracing braid, extending to 7 inches from the bottom of the cuff. Capt: As for Lt, with a row of braided eyes all round the outside of the knot, to an overall height of 8 inches from the bottom of the cuff. Maj – Col: Black 1½-inch lace round the top of the cuff with figured braiding above and below, to an overall height of 11 inches from the bottom of the cuff.

In most orders of dress, officers wore trousers or overalls of rifle green cloth with 2 inch wide stripes of black braid. Boots were black and spurs were steel. The black pouch belt was embellished with a circular silver plate at the top to which a silver whistle was attached by three lengths of silver chain; between the two was a large silver badge, the same as that worn on the helmet except that the ground under the stringed bugle was not voided. On the black patent leather pouch was a silver stringed bugle badge.

99 Lieutenant Colonel King's Royal Rifle Corps circa 1897 (Patrols)

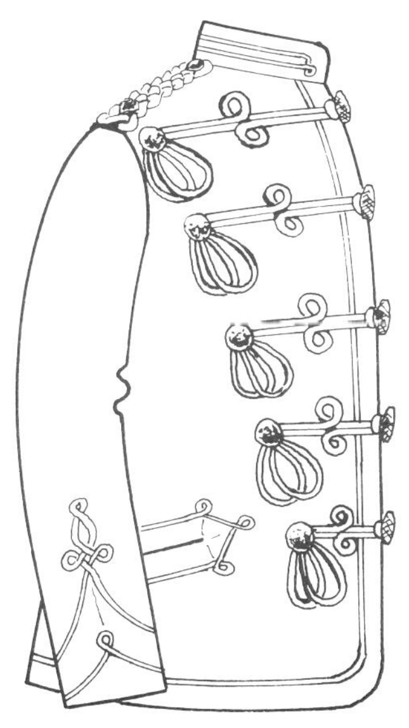

100 *Officer's patrol jacket King's Royal Rifle Corps*

The officer's patrol jacket worn by Simkin's officer was rifle green with scarlet collar and cuffs (see **Figs 99** and **100**); the collar edged all round with ½-inch black braid with an inner edging of black russia braid forming an eye at each end; the cuffs edged with one inch black braid, traced above and below with black russia braid forming a crow's foot and eye above and an eye in the point below; the jacket edged down the front and around the skirts, including the vents, with 1-inch black braid traced inside with black russia braid forming in the centre of the back a plume 6 inches deep below the collar, and a crow's foot and eye above the hem; the back seams covered with 1-inch black braid edged on both sides with black russia braid; five black cord loops and embellishments on the chest as on the tunic (though they are spread out to reach further down – see **Fig 99**).

Cap lines worn by officers with the busby were similar to those worn by officers of Hussars. They were fastened (see **Fig 96**) on the right breast but there seem to have been a variety of ways in which the cord was tied or looped at this point; the reader is encouraged to research further if he wishes to obtain a specific accurate view – and indeed that goes for everything in this book and for that matter in any other publication on this elusive subject!

APPENDIX I

Military Types – Supplements to the Army and Navy Gazette

Note: The list below contains only the first 112 prints covering the Regular Army and Royal Marines. The colour plates in this book have been selected from among the originals for these prints and are located in the right-hand column by the Volume and Plate Number.

NB. This list amends Appendix I to Volume I which should now be disregarded.

No	Title	Published	Index to Originals	
1	1st Life Guards	7 Jan 1888		
2	2nd Life Guards	4 Feb 1888		
3	Royal Horse Guards	3 Mar 1888	Vol 1	No 2
4	1st Dragoon Guards	7 Apr 1888		
5	2nd Dagoon Guards	5 May 1888	Vol 1	No 3
6	3rd Dragoon Guards	2 Jun 1888		
7	4th Dragoon Guards	7 Jul 1888		
8	5th Dragoon Guards	4 Aug 1888		
9	6th Dragoon Guards	1 Sep 1888	Vol 1	No 4
10	7th Dragoon Guards	6 Oct 1888	Vol 1	No 5
11	1st Dragoons	3 Nov 1888	Vol 1	No 6
12	2nd Dragoons	1 Dec 1888	Vol 1	No 7
13	3rd Hussars	5 Jan 1889		
14	4th Hussars	2 Feb 1889	Vol 1	No 13
15	5th Lancers	2 Mar 1889	Vol 1	No 9
16	6th Dragoons	Apr 1889	Vol 1	No 8
17	7th Hussars	4 May 1889		
18	8th Hussars	1 Jun 1889		
19	9th Lancers	6 Jul 1889		
20	10th Hussars	3 Aug 1889		
21	11th Hussars	7 Sep 1889		
22	12th Lancers	5 Oct 1889	Vol 1	No 10
23	13th Hussars	2 Nov 1889		
24	14th Hussars	7 Dec 1889		
25	15th Hussars	4 Jan 1890		
26	16th Lancers	1 Feb 1890	Vol 1	No 11
27	17th Lancers	1 Mar 1890		
28	18th Hussars	5 Apr 1890		
29	19th Hussars	3 May 1890	Vol 1	No 14
30	20th Hussars	7 Jun 1890		
31	21st Hussars	5 Jul 1890	Vol 1	No 15
32	Royal Horse Artillery	2 Aug 1890		
33	Royal Artillery	6 Sep 1890	Vol 1	No 16
34	Royal Engineers	4 Oct 1890	Vol 3	
35	Grenadier Guards	1 Nov 1890	Vol 2	No 1
36	Coldstream Guards	6 Dec 1890	Vol 2	No 2
37	Scots Guards	3 Jan 1891	Vol 2	No 3
38	Royal Scots	7 Feb 1891	Vol 2	No 15
39	The Queen's	7 Mar 1891		
40	The Buffs	4 Apr 1891	Vol 2	No 4
41	Northumberland Fusiliers	2 May 1891	Vol 2	No 5
42	Royal Fusiliers	6 Jun 1891		
43	Somerset Light Infantry	4 Jul 1891		
44	Lancashire Fusiliers	1 Aug 1891		
45	Royal Scots Fusiliers	5 Sep 1891		
46	King's Own Royal Lancashire Regt	3 Oct 1891		
47	Royal Warwickshire Regt	7 Nov 1891		
48	King's Liverpool Regt	5 Dec 1891		
49	Norfolk Regt	2 Jan 1892		
50	Lincolnshire Regt	6 Feb 1892		
51	Devonshire Regt	5 Mar 1892		
52	Suffolk Regt	2 Apr 1892		
53	West Yorkshire Regt	7 May 1892		
54	East Yorkshire Regt	4 Jun 1892		
55	Bedfordshire Regt	2 Jul 1892		
56	Leicestershire Regt	6 Aug 1892		
57	Royal Irish Regt	3 Sep 1892		
58	Yorkshire Regt	1 Oct 1892	Vol 2	No 6
59	Cheshire Regt	5 Nov 1892		
60	Royal Welsh Fusiliers	3 Dec 1892	Vol 2	No 7
61	South Wales Borderers	7 Jan 1893		
62	King's Own Scottish Borderers	4 Feb 1893		
63	Cameronians	4 Mar 1893		
64	Royal Inniskilling Fusiliers	1 Apr 1893	Vol 2	No 8
65	Gloucestershire Regt	6 May 1893		
66	Worcestershire Regt	3 Jun 1893		
67	East Lancashire Regt	1 Jul 1893		
68	East Surrey Regt	5 Aug 1893		
69	Duke of Cornwall's Light Infantry	2 Sep 1893		
70	Duke of Wellington's Regt	7 Oct 1893	Vol 2	No 9
71	Border Regt	4 Nov 1893	Vol 2	No 10
72	Royal Sussex Regt	2 Dec 1893		
73	Hampshire Regt	6 Jan 1894		
74	South Staffordshire Regt	3 Feb 1894		
75	Dorsetshire Regt	3 Mar 1894		
76	South Lancashire Regt	7 Apr 1894		
77	Welsh Regt	5 May 1894		
78	Black Watch	2 Jun 1894		
79	Oxfordshire Light Infantry	7 Jul 1894	Vol 2	No 11
80	Essex Regt	4 Aug 1894		
81	Sherwood Foresters	1 Sep 1894		
82	Loyal North Lancashire Regt	6 Oct 1894		
83	Northamptonshire Regt	3 Nov 1894	Vol 2	No 12
84	Royal Berkshire Regt	1 Dec 1894		
85	Royal Marine Light Infantry	5 Jan 1895	Vol 1	No 18
86	Royal West Kent Regt	2 Feb 1895		
87	King's Own Yorkshire Light Infantry	2 Mar 1895		
88	King's Shropshire Light Infantry	6 Apr 1895		
89	Middlesex Regt	4 May 1895		
90	King's Royal Rifle Corps	1 Jun 1895	Vol 2	No 18
91	Wiltshire Regt	6 Jul 1895	Vol 2	No 13
92	Manchester Regt	3 Aug 1895		
93	North Staffordshire Regt	7 Sep 1895		
94	York and Lancaster Regt	5 Oct 1895		
95	Durham Light Infantry	2 Nov 1895	Vol 2	No 14
96	Highland Light Infantry	7 Dec 1895		
97	Seaforth Highlanders	4 Jan 1896		
98	Gordon Highlanders	1 Feb 1896	Vol 2	No 16
99	Queen's Own Cameron Highlanders	7 Mar 1896	Vol 2	No 17
100	Royal Irish Rifles	4 Apr 1896		
101	Royal Irish Fusiliers	2 May 1896		
102	Connaught Rangers	6 Jun 1896		
103	Argyll and Sutherland Highlanders	4 Jul 1896		
104	Leinster Regt	1 Aug 1896		
105	Royal Munster Fusiliers	5 Sep 1896		
106	Royal Dublin Fusiliers	3 Oct 1896		
107	Rifle Brigade	7 Nov 1896		
108	West India Regt	5 Dec 1896		
109	Army Service Corps	2 Jan 1897		
110	Ordnance Store, Army Pay and Army Veterinary Depts	6 Feb 1897		
111	Army Chaplain, Medical Staff, Hospital Corps and Nursing Sister	6 Mar 1897		
112	Royal Marine Artillery	3 Apr 1897	Vol 1	No 17

APPENDIX II
Abbreviations and Terms

AOs (Army Orders). Orders of general application to the whole Army, though of a less than permanent nature, issued in regular printed batches by the War Office.

Bn (Battalion). A unit of infantry commanded by a Lieutenant Colonel.

BL (Breech-loading). Used to describe a pattern of artillery piece loaded from the rear, or through the breech.

BSM (Battery Sergeant Major). A Staff Sergeant and the senior non-commissioned officer in a battery of artillery.

Bty (Battery). A unit of artillery commanded by a Major and equipped usually, with 6 guns.

Cl (Clause, of Army Orders). The system of numbering Army Orders on various subjects.

CO (Commanding Officer). The senior officer of a unit specifically designated in Orders as empowered to command; usually understood to mean the Lieutenant Colonel Commanding a Regiment (of Cavalry) or Battalion (of Infantry), or unit of another arm of service of equivalent size.

Corps (1) A field formation of all arms commanded by a General. (2) An arm of service, e.g. The Corps of Royal Engineers.

Corps. A term commonly used in the nineteenth century to denote any Regiment, or unit, depending on the context. Not now used in that way.

Coy (Company). A unit or sub-unit, usually of a dismounted arm or service, commanded by a Major if independent or by a Major or a Captain if a sub-unit.

CSgt (Colour Sergeant or Colour Serjeant). In 1890, the senior Sergeant in an Infantry company; in effect he was the Company Sergeant Major.

D Abbreviation for "Dragoons". Used only in the shortened form of a specific Regimental title, e.g. "6 D".

DG Abbreviation for "Dragoon Guards". Used only in the shortened form of a specific Regimental title, e.g. "2 DG".

Dmr (Drummer).

Estb (Establishment). The number of men (and certain items of equipment) authorised by the Government for a given unit. Also used to refer to the document containing this information.

Field Officer Generic term for Majors, Lieutenant Colonels and Colonels on Regimental duty, e.g. commanding a Regimental District.

Frock A loose fitting coat the same length as a tunic but usually with less embellishments.

GO (General Orders). Issued on the authority of the Commander in Chief to govern formal matters.

GOC (General Officer Commanding). An officer of the rank of Major General or above commanding a District or a formation of at least Divisional size.

H Abbreviation for "Hussars". Used only with a numeral in the shortened form of a specific Regimental title, e.g. "4 H".

L Abbriviation for "Lancers". Used only with a numeral in the shortened form of a specific Regimental title, e.g. "5 L".

Line A generic term used to describe those Regiments of the Regular Army which were not part of the Household Cavalry nor the Foot Guards.

NCO (Non-Commissioned Officer). A term used to describe a soldier holding any rank between Lance-Corporal and Staff Sergeant (inclusive), or their equivalents.

Near-side. Relates usually to horses and is the side from which the rider mounts. When he is in the saddle facing forward, it is his (and the horse's) left.

OC (Officer Commanding). The senior officer of a unit or sub-unit specifically designated in Orders as empowered to command; usually understood to refer to a Major commanding an independent unit (e.g. a battery of artillery) or a subordinate sub-unit (e.g. a company of infantry within a battalion) (cf. "CO").

Offr (Officer). This term always means commissioned officers (i.e. Second Lieutenant and above) unless qualified to the contrary.

Off-side. Relates to horses; the animal's right and the opposite of near-side.

OR (Other Rank). All members of the Army not of commissioned rank (i.e. all Warrant Officers and below).

Pdr (pounder). Used only with a numeral (e.g. "12 pdr") to describe the size of an artillery piece, by reference to the weight of its projectile.

Pte (Private). The junior rank in the Army. Common to all Regiments in 1890 except the Household Cavalry (Trooper), Royal Artillery (Gunner) and Royal Engineers (Sapper).

QMS (Quartermaster Sergeant). In 1890, the senior non-commissioned rank below Warrant Officer. It did not then (nor does it now, though its use has changed in other respects) necessarily imply duty of a supply or storekeeping kind.

QRs (Queen's Regulations). A book of orders published by the HQ of the Army at irregular intervals to provide for the command and administration of units and individuals.

RA (Royal Artillery). Used in formal reference to the Royal Regiment of Artillery, though in fact it is an abbreviation itself.

RE (Royal Engineers). Used in formal references to the Corps of Royal Engineers.

Regt (Regiment). (1) A territorial infantry organisation with a common title consisting generally of a depot, two regular battalions, two militia battalions and two or more volunteer battalions. (2) A unit of cavalry commanded by a Lieutenant Colonel.

Remount Term used to describe replacement or reinforcement Army horses between purchase and acceptance into the line.

R&F (Rank and File). Literally refers to that part of a Regiment which was formed up in ranks and files; by 1890, the term was commonly used to refer to Corporals and below only.

RMA (Royal Marine Artillery).

RML (Rifled Muzzle Loading). An artillery system, e.g. the 9- and 13-pounder guns in service in 1890.

RMLI (Royal Marine Light Infantry).

RSM (Regimental Sergeant Major). A Warrant Officer and the senior non-commissioned rank in a regiment of cavalry, a battalion of infantry, or a unit of another arm or service of equivalent size.

Russia braid. If not flat, the section of all braid is usually specifically described in Dress Regulations and elsewhere, with one exception. This is russia braid which is made of plaited metal wire or worsted and looks like twin electric flex. It is $\frac{1}{8}$ inch wide unless specified otherwise and is fastened to the garment, etc. with a single line of stitching along the channel between the two "cords".

Sabretache A leather case with pockets for papers and pencils worn by mounted soldiers and secured by leather slings to the sword belt.

Sgt or Sjt (Serjeant). A non-commissioned rank between Corporal and Staff Serjeant.

Shabraque A saddle cloth. The term was usually only applied to the richly ornamented variety.

Sqn (Squadron). A sub-unit of a mounted arm usually commanded by a Major and consisting of 100–150 men.

SSgt (Staff Sergeant or Staff Serjeant). In 1890, a rank above Sgt held by certain non-commissioned officers on the HQ of a regiment or battalion. The "Staff" in this instance relates to the unit HQ staff. (Note that the form is used quite differently today.)

Str (Strength). The number of men (or animals, etc.) actually "on the books" of the unit or formation in question. This is not to be confused with the establishment.

Subaltern. A generic term which describes officers holding the rank of 2nd Lieutenant or Lieutenant.

Sub-unit. A military organisation, usually of company or squadron size, or smaller, which is part of a larger organisation (or unit) upon which it depends for command and administration.

Tp (Troop). A sub-unit of a mounted arm usually commanded (in 1890) by a Major or a Captain and consisting of about 50–75 men.

Tpr (Trooper). The lowest rank in The Household Cavalry; equated to Private in the Foot Guards and the Line.

Trump (Trumpeter).

Tunic. A closely fitted uniform coat cut with skirts. It was usually the full dress garment and may be compared with the looser frock.

Unit. A military organisation commanded by an officer usually not below the rank of major in RA and RE, and usually not below Lieutenant Colonel in other arms. A unit is the smallest military organisation permitted an independent administrative existence, i.e. its commander has the powers of a CO as defined in Queen's Regulations and he may operate his own accounts.

WO (Warrant Officer). A rank between NCOs and officers. There were a number of grades of WO ranging from Conductor at the top down to Regimental Sergeant Major and Bandmaster among the more junior. (cf. battery Sergeant Major and also note that Troop Sergeant Major was an appointment held by an NCO of the rank of Staff Sergeant.)

APPENDIX III
Bibliography

(1) "A British Officer". Social Life in the British Army. (John Long, London, 1900)

(2) Bowling A H. British Hussar Regiments. (Almark Publishing Co Ltd, New Malden, 1972)

(3) Carman W Y. British Military Uniforms from Contemporary Pictures. (Leonard Hill, London, 1957)

(4) Carman W Y. Headdresses of the British Army – Cavalry. (W Y Carman, Sutton, 1968)

(5) Cooper-King Col C. The British Army and Auxiliary Forces. (Cassell, London, 1893)

(6) Dawnay Maj N P. The Badges of Warrant and Non-Commissioned Rank in the British Army. (Society for Army Historical Research Special Publication No 6)

(7) Field Col C. Britian's Sea Soldiers (2 volumes). (Lyceum Press, Liverpool, 1923)

(8) Fraser E and Carr-Laughton L G. The Royal Marine Artillery 1804–1923 (2 volumes). (Royal United Services Institution, London, 1930)

(9) Goodenough Lt Col W H and Dalton Lt Col J C. The Army Book for the British Empire (HMSO, London, 1893)

(10) Kipling A L and King H L. Headdress Badges of the British Army. (Frederick Muller Ltd, London, 1972)

(11) Leslie N B. The Battle Honours of the British and Indian Armies. (Leo Cooper Ltd, London, 1970)

(12) Parkyn H G. Shoulder-Belt Plates and Buttons. (Gale and Polden, Aldershot, 1956)

(13) Perry O L. Rank and Badges . . . in her Majesty's Army and Navy and Auxiliary Forces. (W Clowes and Sons, London 1888)

(14) Robinson Cdr C M (Ed). Navy and Army Illustrated. (A magazine published from 1895 by George Newnes Ltd, London)

(15) Robinson Cdr C N (Ed). The Transvaal War Album. (George Newnes Ltd, London nd (*c.*1900))

(16) Stadden C. The Life Guards (Almark Publishing Co Ltd, New Malden, 1971)

(17) Swinson A. A Register of the Regiments and Corps of the British Army. (Archive Press Ltd, London, 1972)

(18) Tylden Maj G. Horses and Saddlery. (Army Museums Ogilby Trust)

(19) Tylden Maj G. Discovering Harness and Saddlery (No 119 in the Discovering series, Shire Publications, Aylesbury, 1971 and 1979)

(20) War Office/HMSO
    Army Estimates for 1890/91
    Army List 1890
    Army Orders
    Cavalry Regulations 1887
    Clothing Regulations 1887
    Dress Regulations 1883 (as amended)
    Equipment Regulations 1881
    General Monthly Return(s) of the Regimental Strength of the British Army 1877 Handbook for 9pdr Rifled ML Gun
    Handbook for 12pdr BL Gun Mk I Land Service 1891
    Infantry Drill 1889
    Lists of Changes 1860–1890
    Queen's Regulations 1889

(21) Wilkinson-Latham R. Swords in Colour. (Blandford Press Ltd, Poole, 1977)

(22) Carman W Y. Richard Simkin's Uniforms of the British Army (Webb & Bower, Exeter, 1982 (Cavalry) and 1985 (Infantry))

(23) Chichester H M and Burges-Short G. The Records and Badges of . . . the British Army. (Gale and Polden, Aldershot, 1900; facsimile reprint by Frederick Muller, London, 1970)

(24) Edwards D and Langley D. British Army Proficiency Badges (Wardley Publishing, Prestatyn, 1984)

(25) Farmer J S. Regimental Records of the British Army (Grant Richards 1901; reprint by Crecy Books, Bristol, 1984)

(26) The Scottish Division. Regiments of the Scottish Division (Macmillan, London, 1979)

(27) Smith D J. Discovering Horse Drawn Transport of the British Army (No 233 in the Discovering series, Shire Publications, Aylesbury, 1977)

(28) Stadden C. Coldstream Guards (Almark Publishing Co Ltd, New Malden, 1973)

THE PLATES

Grenadier Guards
Officer and Other Ranks

Coldstream Guards
Officer and Other Ranks

Scots Guards
Officer and Other Ranks

Buffs (East Kent Regiment)
Officer and Other Ranks

Northumberland Fusiliers
Officer and Other Ranks

Princess of Wales's Own (Yorkshire) Regiment
Lieutenant Colonel and Sergeant Major

Royal Welsh Fusiliers
Officer and Sergeant Drummer

Royal Inniskilling Fusiliers
Officers and Other Ranks

Duke of Wellington's (West Riding) Regiment
Officers and Drummer

Border Regiment
Sergeant Drummer and Drummer

Oxfordshire Light Infantry
Officer and Other Ranks

Northamptonshire Regiment
Lieutenant Colonel and Drummer

Duke of Edinburgh's (Wiltshire Regiment)
Officer and Other Ranks

Durham Light Infantry
Officer and Other Ranks

Royal Scots (The Lothian Regiment)
Officer and Other Ranks

Gordon Highlanders
Officer and Other Ranks

Queen's Own Cameron Highlanders
Officer and Other Ranks

King's Royal Rifle Corps
Officer and Other Ranks